ISBN-13: 978-1492374220
ISBN-10: 1492374229
ASIN: B00F2ISBWO

Original Edition Published
09·11·13 Backscatter Media
BACK·126

Written & Produced by Trevor Weeks
between January 2012 & July 213
Cover art & book layout by Trevor Weeks

Inquiries?
http://taweeks.com

RESONANT

BY

TREVOR WEEKS

3

for
amanda

Ch. 1
| foundation |

"Rise and shine sleepy" she said. My lab partner Emily was always a bit too perky for eight AM. I was only barely able to make out her playful smile as she turned to see if I would wake up.

Peeling my head off my desk and beginning to feel the pins and needles from my sleeping leg; I hastily began gathering my laptop and the other extraneous clutter I had brought to my music theory class. Professor Hyden didn't seem to care much or even notice his last student leaving through the heavy double doors.

I had my headphones on before I left the building. Bach wasn't doing it for me on my bee line to grab some espresso, so instead of trying to mirror my mood, I broke the mirror in favor of a little Prodigy to give the coffee a head start. It seemed like everyone was driving like they had a death wish on the way back to my apartment, but it also may have been one of those point of view things in hind sight.

The sticking lock on my front door let me know that Mr. Carter the maintenance man is still working on Mrs. Carroll's *plumbing*, apparently a matter of priorities.

I lived alone and I liked it that way. The rent was cheap, the lighting scarce and the bare concrete walls gave off a somehow nostalgic air that subtlety permeated everything in the small space.

There was not much there that I didn't need. In my mind, I am a minimalist for all intents and purposes, but somehow that never seemed to be my reality despite constant efforts to the contrary. My thoughts are clear and distilled; only the outside world clouds and complicates them.

There's something about silence that comforts more than alienates me; and with that thought I flipped on the overloaded power strip that brought to life the menagerie of cords, adapters, wires and jerry-rigged connectors that all led into an otherwise empty storage closet. The closet had long ago traded the mediocrity of standard grey concrete in lieu of a dry, white alien landscape that covered every crack and surface in the tiny room.

To touch it was soft and smooth like a baby's bottom, but its chalky residue carried only a trace of its former non-Newtonian glory. It was dried corn starch. This was the latest toy I had been playing with. In the right proportions, the corn starch and water mixture would writhe and dance in the most peculiar and drunken ways when acted upon by various sound frequencies that were precisely controlled by the slew of electronics hooked up to the unfortunate subwoofer cone that briefly housed this substance before it walks or jumps out, seemingly autonomously until the power's cut and its soul escapes.

I mixed up a fresh batch of the stubborn liquid and proceeded to put it on its dance floor and started the camcorder I had setup to record certain behaviors I was tracking at various frequencies. At very low frequencies, it was fascinating to watch the cymatic patterns forming that were to me, unequivocal proof of creationism. This was something that I could experience with all of my senses and as cold and scientific as it was, filled me with a warm inner light. The sensation wasn't something I could necessarily describe or prove, but it was something that began tickling a lot of different connections in my mind and it felt like the tension when two magnets are about to snap together in perfect polarity.

It reminded me of the beginning of the bible in genesis where it says "And God said, "Let there be light," and there was light." I think of this quite literally, that there was sound from the spirit of God, *then* there was light and all matter that followed.

The answer to many unknowns is hidden, but not everything is so cryptic, it's a matter of recognizing something for what it literally is and other times it may need to be deciphered further.

I proceeded to marginally increase the amplitude and frequency of the signal that was giving meaning and life to the viscous substance over the next 15 minutes or so until it had completely disseminated to the walls like its former comrades. I did this a couple of more times that night to finish charting the other frequencies I wanted to explore.

I caught some great images and afterward, went to my computer to extract and analyze them. As usual, my inbox was full of unanswered messages and the ever punctual deluge of spam. I decided it was time to do a quick purge, but one email caught my attention; the subject read "Thank a Soldier."

Most people have no idea what patriotic means, thinking that forwarding patriotic motivational chain-spam, lighting fireworks and voting while stuffing your face with hotdogs and coke is patriotism.

Now, don't get me wrong, I love my country as much as anyone could and deeply respect the personal sacrifice they are making, but I can't help but feel it's more than a little misguided.

When it comes to dissecting why we have wars in the first place, there are more than a few shady areas. Think what would be possible if there was no greed and power lust.

This is an obviously flawed and overly optimistic hypothetical, but if those two engrained human characteristics so prevalent in some of the world's most powerful people did not exist, we would have a much different global outlook and current state of affairs to deal with.

Since we do not live in any kind of ideal like that, we have to be open to the absolute that there will always be people that will want more power and more money. I've found the statement "power corrupts, but absolute power corrupts absolutely" to be true, time and time again from personal observation and from the expertly crafted history books I've read. Reading between the lines has always been paramount to grasping an understanding of the true nature of things.

There are so many things that just don't make sense. So much distortion and disinformation has been pummeling us from every direction for our entire lives that most people have become immune to even realize the waves are hitting them, some visible, most in hidden, secret combinations.

Our earth and we as a collective human race have more than enough time, money and resources to make sure that there is no one that could want for anything, but through thousands of years refining the art of maintaining control over the majority by a select few that hoard knowledge, money and power, we have given away most of our rights for a false sense of security from those who claim to be protecting us.

There could not be a more blatant example of a wolf in sheep's clothing. Events like 9/11 or other domestic terror attacks, whether you believe they were inside jobs or not, are gateway events that cause real policy changes in every aspect of human life globally. They provide an opportunity for world leaders to propagate changes, often pushing through old, rewritten legislation in a relevant and somewhat publically digestible form, using catastrophic events as springboards to green light laws that would never have been passed in a world before a given tragedy.

Why would we as patriotic Americans trade sacred freedoms that this country was founded upon and that so many heroic men and women have fought and died for? The answer is tiringly simple.

Fear is the easiest human emotion to prey upon, the most primal of our negative emotions to which we respond instinctively to with a survivalist mentality. When we or our loved ones or our hard-earned assets are threatened, we do *whatever is necessary* to protect that which we hold dear, the powers that be are keenly aware of this and exploit that to no end for their power and financial benefit.

They too are in a kind of survivalist mode as they are not immune to fear either; they just have a fear of losing power and money, not their basic freedom like the rest of the global population. Fear is a powerful weapon and it is used in that way on many levels, but it is still not the most powerful emotion that can affect us, the most powerful and effective emotion we can use to counter any obstacle is love.

I know it sounds cliché, but it's a cliché for a reason; love conquers all. Love for ourselves and for our fellow humans is the basest mindset and way of acting that can bring about real change, even if we have to fight to love. This is not a subject I take lightly or think anyone else should take lightly as it affects us all and every human has certain rights that should never be compromised.

The problem that everyone faces is the lack of organization behind a true cause. The fear that paralyzes everyone has been carefully exercised over our human race since the beginning of civilization by those in power. I felt the same way for as long as I could remember. I felt lost, helpless, hopeless and just wishing someone would do something to turn this mess of a world around. I was not alone in this darkness, not by a longshot.

The next day was my day off and I had set a goal to not feel obligated to do anything. With this rare freedom of time, I decided to take a trip down to the fresh fish market in hopes of scoring a nice piece of Hamachi for the sushi I planned on making for dinner that evening. I hopped on my mountain bike and headed on the half hour ride down to Fulton's. It was a little busier than usual that day, but I was still in and out pretty quickly with a choice fillet on ice that was calling my name.

I began my ride back home loving the fast, warm air rushing over my face, arms and legs; a very liberating feeling compared to my usual prescription of fluorescent sunshine most days. Just before I arrived home, I received a call from my friend Lars, reminding me of my long-standing commitment to help him move today. After silently cursing myself out, I let him know I'd be there within the hour.

I couldn't help but notice the sky as I talked with Lars. Gridlocked residual chem-trails have been infecting our sky for years, a sinister reminder of things left unquestioned, something I'd been growing increasingly more aware of over the past few years. What I found strange was that anyone I'd ever asked about them looked at me like I was speaking a foreign language, like they had never noticed anything out of the ordinary.

I'd been watching them appear in the sky since my childhood and remembered noticing the difference between contrails and chem-trails, the long lasting and obviously artificial chem-trails pretended to be clouds. They had become much more frequent, especially the past few years, traversing the sky latitudinally and longitudinally like they were getting ready to play a giant game of tic-tac-toe.

It was undeniably systematic. After a few hours, the lines would fade and drift into what can only be described as a misty haze of a cloud that would appear to join with the smog by the next day, nothing like the majesty of the mighty Cumulonimbus and nothing like this nasty little reminder to put a rain cloud over my day.

I tried to shake off the past few minutes and realign my thoughts to be more positive, after all, I had a delectable delicacy waiting as my reward at the end of the day. After stopping by home to drop my dinner off in the fridge, I started on my way over to help Lars.

From a few blocks away, I could see heavy congestion around Central Park where a large crowd had been gathering and police were beginning to arrive and systematically disseminate to form what looked like a fairly large perimeter, posting officers at strategic crowd control points. Besides the militant but unprovoked police presence, everything seemed to be relatively calm.

After getting a bit closer to the action and talking with a guy there, he told me the reason this group had gathered was for a non-violent gathering of several hundred people protesting against the acquittal of a major insider trading lawsuit brought against multi billionaire tycoon and C.E.O. of NanoCell Intl. Conrad Vanderbilt who had just been cleared of any wrong doing in a scandal which ended up costing the shareholders of his company's stock and the city (i.e. taxpayers) hundreds of millions of dollars and in turn was able to personally capitalize as the sole beneficiary of those funds.

Needless to say, he was not a popular man on this day in this place. Maneuvering further through the crowd of zealous protesters which was only diversified by SWAT personnel and media vehicles by this point, I tried to get a little closer to where the central makeshift platform which raised its frustrated speakers off the ground only a couple of feet.

Fed up citizens took turns rallying each other by taking turns speaking about the details of the injustice that had recently played out and how it affected them. Each person brought up a different point about what kind of an impact this meant for various city projects that would have to be cut because of the money the city lost in the process. People were very upset about the impact it would have on schools, public transportation, libraries and hospitals and other city-subsidized arts programs; the list went on and on with people voicing their opinions with desperate passion and genuine concern.

As people would speak, the crowd seemed to be feeding off its own energy, it seemed like people were getting worked up about the issues more and more as the protest evolved. One middle aged man got up and started talking about how his father was a WWII & Korean War vet and was a devoted member of his local VFW chapter and becoming even more active since his late wife had passed. The VFW was already short on funds and with subsidized funding being threatened to be cut now, his father would have nothing left in his world to keep him going.

He was successful in communicating just how much this meant to his dad to the buzzing crowd. When people would bring up special needs groups like that and kids and community programs that would really tug on their heartstrings. This wasn't necessarily about this specific verdict that was read earlier that day; it was about a lot more than that. People in general had a very bad taste in their mouths from this, unemployment, the way the government had been running and a lot of other issues that had clearly been coming to a boil.

The man was still talking about his veteran father, about how "he served his country for 37 years and this is how he's repaid?" I meant no disrespect to him and I have no idea what possessed me other than the contagious electricity of the crowd working through me, but I blurted out an answer to his rhetorical question. I said "at least he came back" I immediately became acutely aware that I had said that a little louder than I thought and felt all eyes and eager TV camera lenses shift their gravity to focus on me.

There was not one light hearted countenance in the sea of faces and I had never felt such tension. I paused for just a moment while time seemed to stand still followed by what felt like a bolt of lightning erupt through and out of me. I felt it rip through my body at the speed of light and I could physically feel it annihilating all of my insecure negativity and purge it instantly. I felt intensely alive, all of my senses were heightened and I could feel a connective energy with everyone there. It was surreal and exhilarating.

I moved quickly and politely toward the soapbox where the man was still visibly concerned about what I had just said. He kept his eyes locked on me and said nothing while stepping down like a wolf that had just lost his alpha position, cautiously submitting. I stepped up on the micro stage. I opened my mouth and it was as if I was merely a vessel for what I began saying.

"I'm sure he is a great man and we all owe him our respect, but what about all the millions of other great men than have left their wife, their children and their lives to fight in unjust wars for old rich white men and died in vein? No VFW clubhouse or pension will ever be enough compensation for what is taken from a victim of war, if he makes it out alive and certainly not if he doesn't.

Men like Conrad Vanderbilt are cut from the same cloth as the rest of the elite in power now and historically, they are blood profiteers. They view people like a commodity like cattle or even worse, like a liability. Men like this are in business to gain money and power and treat human life like pawns on their chessboard. The golden rule is those that have the gold make the rules. They can do what they want, when they want and no one ever dares stand in their way.

They hire hoards of lawyers and lobbyists to push anything they want through congress and find loopholes to exploit every system they want to manipulate, successfully! They do whatever they can to lie to us, to get us to spend all of our meager wages back on the products they sell that contain poisons of every kind, they cause hyperinflation by destabilizing the markets and printing more and more money with wages never going up in the process. Everyone is forced spend more and but they don't make more when prices go up. They regulate oil prices, they give out stimulus money knowing that most Americans are forced to use it to pay off old debt or have such broken financial spirits and will turn around and spend that money back to the same corporations that are all part of this mess.

That money is being withdrawn from the privately owned federal reserve which loaned stimulus money to the government and we taxpayers not only have to pay back the loan, but with a ridiculous amount of interest, so we end up footing the bill, twice. Corporate-hired politicians appoint their Wall Street fat cat cronies to head up the treasury and run the Federal Reserve; am I the only one who feels like this could be a conflict of interest?

They secretly embezzle trillions of dollars and funnel it into countless black projects under various unassuming umbrella departments like FEMA and the Department of Energy and so on.

They coerced us into trading our civil liberties, basic human freedoms and privacy by passing Homeland Security after 9/11, what makes any one of you think that they will not keep pushing the envelope just like this? There is a trending history here that spares no culture or demographic.

I hope everyone noticed how I'm speaking about corporate business and our government synonymously, they are one and the same. Just as the lines between government and corporate are blurred to the point of non-existence, so are the lines of political parties, all an illusion meant to distract and divide. This is the original World Wide Web, a nasty tangled network that is indelibly intertwined in corruption and greed mongering.

Some say youth is wasted on the young, today I think it can be said that wealth is wasted on these rich thugs. They make secret oaths in their secret societies and perform satanic rituals with political implications. I mean, how far down this rabbit hole do you want to go? Where do you draw the line? When is enough, enough?"

With this, there was an eruption of cheering and yelling, a battle cry, in stark contrast to the reverence I was shown during my rant. I didn't know where all this was coming from inside me. I had done my research over the years and generally kept up on current global events, but I hadn't ever really talked to anyone about it for fear of being mocked by someone who couldn't carry the conversation. This was not that, this was alive; this was hope on a massive scale.

People are smarter and more in tune than they realize. They are typically just distracted by their lives, by design. I had so much more to say, I felt rejuvenated and ready to take on the world and so did everyone there. Everyone was cheering and waving their fists in the air. By this time the crowd had tripled and so had the police presence. Maybe they could tell this would not go down completely peacefully or maybe it was planned because just then a single gunshot was fired that seemed to have come from the crowd and not the perimeter where the police were stationed.

This briefly shocked everyone and excited them at the same time causing a pushing frenzy by a few panicked people which quickly led into a full scale riot. There was chaos everywhere; people began running and ruining everything they could get their hands on, dumping trash cans, breaking windows, even capsizing police cars.

I tried yelling to get everyone's attention to stop, but by this point we had passed the event horizon. Fights between police and protesters broke out and many people were being arrested. This is when I realized it was a good time to be on my way. Trying to push my way out of the eye of the tornado was almost successful until I was tackled by an officer and assertively held down by a hard knee pad to the spine and a very angry voice letting me know I was under arrest for "inciting a riot" I don't remember much after the nightstick to the back of my head.

Ch. 2
| splendor |

I awoke to the reeking smell of some kind of synthetic fuel in a dimly lit space that I could only describe as a huge human kennel. The air was warm and humid, not from water moisture but humid from whatever chemical I was smelling; it was thick and felt like I was wearing it, like a weightless plasma tracksuit.

My head didn't hurt nearly as much as I thought it should, especially considering the fair amount of dried blood on the back of my shirt collar. I was the only tenant in one of the hundreds of three by eight foot cages. They were made of a very thick gauge steel wire in a large mesh pattern, all the walls were concrete. I was sure of two things by this point; this was not the police station and I was not in Kansas anymore. It was very quiet for a very long time.

Across town, Candace Vanerbilt had been paying close attention to the people protesting against her father, she was not one to miss an opportunity to passive-aggressively mock his latest crucible. She was studying linguistics and ancient anthropology at Columbia University at the time, to the great dismay of her father. He dismissed her research as "an old fools work with no practical implications in the real world,"

but this was nothing new as he had made a lifetime hobby of demeaning her choices and actions, she always saw disappointment in his eyes. Growing up the only child of the world's richest man, Candace wanted for nothing her entire life, unless you count approval and affection from her compassionately dead father.

He had spent his entire life building and expanding his corporate empire and was a fanatical workaholic. She spent most of her childhood being primped and shuttled around by the legion of staff her parents had amassed to help maintain and micro manage every detail of her waking day.

Now 24, she is top of her class riding her own scholarship ticket, but still living with her parents in their massive Penthouse in lower Manhattan. Candace had been revisiting the protest videos online in the days following to see the extraordinary events that had just taken place and she wasn't the only one. In less than a week the video had become the epitome of viral, approaching 100 million views. People had definitely taken notice; this had mixed implications to say the least. The buzz had grown so much that after countless attempts from the media and every other walk of life to contact me with no success, people began asking questions and pressuring the police department for answers as to my arrest details.

It was desolate in the six sided cell I called home for what seemed like months without any light change. There was a constant low buzz coming from the endless rows of fluorescent tube lights that emitted a dim, pale green light. There was nothing in the cell except an open, black, four inch round PVC pipe sticking out of the concrete about two feet tall on one end of the cell which I had to assume was a latrine of sorts and subsequently forced to use it as such.

On the opposite end of the human trap was what looked like a bank teller send tube, this was how food and drinks were sent to and taken from me, twice daily. The most terrifying part of this ordeal was the complete lack of human contact. I heard nothing and saw no one; in a facility that looked to have been equipped to hold hundreds of people like this.

Two weeks after the riot, public pressure had become so immense that the police chief was forced to finally issue a statement saying that I was to be released the following day. When the time came, a door about fifty feet away from my cell cracked open and three men emerged from a contrastingly white light. They were all dressed black from head to toe, two of them were clearly identifiable as guards with their black BDU's and laser sighted assault rifles not unlike the SWAT team I was arrested by, but they had no markings of any kind on their uniforms and were wearing red-lensed safety glasses with a slew of other high tech gadgets visible on them.

The third man was in full surgical scrubs including a mask and cap layered with a lab coat, all black except for a small red embroidered symbol above his heart on the lab coat. I had never seen the foreign looking symbol before; it looked like a circle with a triangle inside of the circle, pointing downward. Inside the triangle was a cursive looking letter "T."

One of the guards shone an incapacitating blue light at my face which seemed to come from a device no larger than a palm-sized Maglite. I was completely aware and coherent although completely paralyzed where I stood. I sent the signal from my brain to my hand to move... nothing, same with my voice. I was still able to see, hear and feel and with heightened senses. It reminded me of dreams I had as a child where I would be hit with a clear blue light before floating from my bed out of the window.

I was helpless in every sense of the word as the thin doctor sunk a very large hollow syringe in behind my right earlobe. He depressed the small button on the end of the device which firmly implanted something sharp inside my skull. I felt it bite down and quickly, but painfully settle inside me. My implanter briskly exited alone as I was still being mysteriously restrained by the cool blue light while the less involved guard began to give me very terse directions of where we'd be walking, further impressing on me that it would very much be in my best interest to follow his instructions to a "T" I didn't doubt him under the circumstances. The other guard switched off the blue light device that had been freezing me like a statue for the past few minutes and they both led me out of the cell.

As we walked down the oppressively lit corridor, one guard walked on my right side while the other walked impendingly behind us. I was led through another set of heavy doors, then through another twisting corridor and finally through a very high tech automated door which seemed to scan us as we passed through based on the beeping and electronic noises I heard as we entered. This led us into a very large room with many doors, however with relatively low ceilings compared to the rest of the facility's twenty-foot ceilings.

This room was all concrete and steel from what I could see, but painted black. The only thing that seemed odd was the fact that there were various colored horizontal stripes about three inches thick spanning the width of each door at eye level. The stripes were more than paint as the solid lines were broken up on the left most portion of the stripe, becoming what looked very similar to a vertical bar code pattern.

Beyond this, I did not see any other discerning marks. I was led through the door with the yellow line which opened up into a tunnel that had been carved through raw earth. The rock walls were inlaid with horizontal row of flood lights, it felt very dank like a cave. We walked down a slight ramp onto a platform that was directly in front of an open door to what looked like some kind of airstream, pill bug shuttle, even armored with over lapping plates like that which seemed aerodynamic as well as protective. The guards gestured for me to sit down in the futuristic vehicle as the sole passenger.

I quickly obliged as I didn't see a better alternative. As I settled into the chair, I was automatically strapped in and tightly secured by a multi-point safety harness. The sound of the sliding door closing was followed up by the sound of pressurized gas being released into the cabin. Seconds later my eyelids became too heavy to hold open. I drifted off to sleep feeling terrified as it was not by choice.

I awoke in yet another cell some time later, but it was clear I was in a police station at this point as everything was now recognizable. When a nearby guard noticed I was waking up, he left and quickly returned with the police chief who opened my cell and said with a very stern face but soft and low voice

"you're luckier than you know today son."

He opened the cell door and politely gestured for me to leave "You're free to go, watch yourself" he said as the original guard escorted me out of the holding area and out through the department offices to a mob of impatiently waiting media scum barking copious amounts of indiscernible questions at me.

The sheer volume and intensity of the frenzied reporters clicking and whirring their electronic devices in my face was so intense that I became disoriented, like a bad dream I couldn't wake up from. I had to physically push my way through the doors and out of the building.

The reporters followed me as I headed down the stairs of the station where I was also met by an insurmountable number of bystanders who had apparently come to see my release. At first sighting of me, there was huge roaring cheer from hundreds of people that had come to show their support for my unjust incarceration.

I was confused, disoriented, tired, upset, but mostly overwhelmed. I wasn't here to make a speech; I just wanted to get out of this mess and fast. There was a polished black

Mercedes parked at the bottom of the stairs. About halfway down the stairs, a very attractive young woman frantically beckoned to me

"Asher, come quickly, I can help!"

I almost couldn't make out what she said because of the crowd's volume and I think she sensed this as well and repeated herself just in case. Psychologically inundated, I made a bee line to the pristine German sedan in a panicked attempt to escape the mass of confusion surrounding me. I glanced in the car first and saw only the girl inside. Against my better judgment, I jumped into the open back door and slammed it shut as I nearly fell over sideways onto my heroin.

The driver sped off as I began to collect myself and we awkwardly laughed to each other in relief of our escape.

"Hi, I'm Candace by the way"

she spoke in a soft endearing voice.

"Asher"

I replied. She began to say something, but I interrupted,

"So, how is it that you know my name and why were all those people there?"

"Everyone knows your name. You've been all over the news and the internet for the past two weeks."

she said.

"Two weeks!"

I blurted out.

"I've been gone for two weeks?"

She continued to explain to me the implications of what I had said before the riot.

"The riots are the least of what's happened, it's what you said and how you said it that has inspired so many people and lit a fire under their asses. We need a change and the world knows it, some of us have known for longer than others, but we are united with the idea now, thanks to you. People look up to you now, more than you know, they have been waiting for you and so have I. You have a responsibility because you are their voice"

I snapped at her

"I'm not anyone's voice but my own, I don't even really remember what I said. I'm only one person and was just thinking out loud, next thing I know, I'm waking up caged in a cell."

She could tell I was distraught and in a bad place. She quickly apologized and we sat in silence for a couple of minutes, both looking out opposing windows, until I asked he to drop me off at home. She nodded to the driver who was watching for her queue after the question I pose, the driver complied and turned toward my apartment.

We arrived shortly after as it was not far. I thanked her for the ride, as I went for the door handle she politely touched my hand and said "please call me if you need anything, anything at all, I want to help."

She handed me a scrap of paper with just a phone number on it. I gave her a half smile as turned to walk up the steps to my apartment. When I arrived at my front door, the fact that I did not have my keys or wallet didn't matter because the front door wasn't locked, it wasn't even shut. There was no sign of break in on the door; it was just slightly ajar.

Not knowing what or who was waiting for me inside, I cautiously pushed the door open and crept into my own place like a thief in the night. My belongings had been thoroughly looked through and picked over. All of my equipment, books, computers and everything electronic was gone and the detritus that was left minimal at best. Only a few common household items and clothes shrouded my cheap furniture and floors.

Even personal effects had been ravaged and taken. I immediately exited the shell of my home and headed straight down to Mr. Carter's apartment to ask him if he had seen anything. I banged on his door, clearly interrupting his flavor of the week maintenance work with whatever floozy he had in there.

"Hey, this is Asher from 309, you seen anyone in my place lately?"

He replied with

"hey man, I'm busy in here"

This only fueled my fire. I kicked his door as hard as I could and said

"This is serious, did you see anything?"

I heard a scuffle and a woman sigh. He came to the door wearing a blanket like a toga and said

"yeah man, I saw a bunch of cops in there, they said they had a warrant and left with a bunch of your stuff"

I was seething and stomped off like teen angst. He yelled after me as I left saying

"but they looked like SWAT or something, sorry man."

I went back to my apartment to scrounge for change to buy a few credits for a phone call. I found enough for a few credits between the couch cushions and went around the corner to the mini mart's ComBooth to call Candace. I pulled the scrap of paper from my back right pocket and dialed.

"Hello" a recently familiar voice said on the other end, again

"hello"

I paused for a few moments, not knowing what to say. I finally mustered enough gumption to speak.

"I need to talk to you"

Candace immediately knew it was me. She said

"okay, good, but not on the phone, I'll pick you up at your place in ten minutes."

I agreed and went back to my building to wait on the steps. She was there in half the expected time. I got in and we were driven to Central Park. Candace didn't say anything on the ride over and I assumed we weren't talking in the car for a reason. We got out and walked around the baseball fields on the north end of the park and found a place to sit and talk on one of the dugout benches.

She pulled her phone out and had a video queued up already, it was of me saying my piece at the rally just before the riot. I was surprised at what I was seeing; it didn't sound or look like me. I was just pissed and venting my feelings. It just seemed natural at the time but gave me a completely foreign feeling watching it now. The video had over 250 million views by this point.

She proceeded to show me the myriad of websites that had cropped up just in the last two weeks as well as the other existing sites of the same nature that had shifted focus to me and what I had said. The websites and forums we're alive with the buzz of disgust for the government and major corporations who were now heavily dubbed

"enemies of the people."

There was an unmistakably clear tone of disdain   powered   by   thousands   upon

33

thousands of unanswered questions about the shady behavior of these entities covered up over the years in the name of national security and economic growth. This time-honored, nonchalant attitude toward the public was now decidedly taboo and quickly coming to a head, along with my sanity and my ability to understand how this got blown out of proportion and why I was being targeted for a few things I said in haste at a protest rally.

I expressed this frustration over the next hour or so with Candace and she did the same, just a solid exchange of ideas. It was a truly humble, human and honest interaction between two people. It went from very frustrated to very open and cathartic over this hour, then we dug a little deeper, getting on the subject of her family and coming to know exactly who she was and how tremendously wealthy her father was.

I began to question to myself about what her motivation was to even be talking to me, she was inextricably tied and even bound by blood to the very person that started me down this path and whom I felt had something to do with my detainment and illegal search and seizure, but didn't have any proof.

Sensing my uneasiness in the conversation at this point, she did her best to explain her conflicted feelings about her family and her father in particular, but if she hadn't disclaimed her statement beforehand, I would have thought for sure that she and her father were mortal enemies. I had rarely seen such a great clash of principle and point of view of the world than the difference between she and her father; she was the perfect antithesis of him in every conceivable way.

We talked for another hour or so about corporate America, politics, the media, conservation, off-the-grid living, animal and human rights and somehow landed on the subject of love and how important it was in general and how the simple lacking of love had caused do much wrong in the world. We discussed how her father never showed her any love and how she thinks it was because his parents never showed him love either, but he had never told her much about the circumstances of his childhood other than the general sentiment that kids have it extremely easy these days compared to his childhood.

The old adage

"the apple never falls far from the tree"

that usually proved true showed no signs of holding any weight in this case. We had one of those perfectly flowing conversations that you never want to end, such a harmonious ebb and flow was rare for me. We started walking back to the car where her driver was still patiently waiting for us. We talked about getting coffee, until I realized I didn't have any credits. She offered me coffee back at her place and I gratefully agreed since we had been getting along so well and we both wanted to keep on talking.

The driver pulled into a private garage entrance through a lift gate, then in through another overhead garage door to what looked like a mini car museum. It was filled with a very random assortment of classic and exotic vehicles from the last 100 years and from all corners of the globe. Candace was not slow to notice that my man-interest had been piqued by all this beautiful machinery I suddenly found myself surrounded by.

She was patient and said

"feel free to look around"

as she gestured me to look at anything I wanted. I soon found myself face to face with a very rare 1961 Porsche RS61 Spyder, my childhood dream car. I had to check to make sure I wasn't drooling too obviously. We finished up looking in the garage after a few minutes and headed toward the elevator, we both stepped inside and she pressed the "P" button, not for parking, but for penthouse.

From the outside in the parking garage the elevator was nondescript, a common freight elevator, but inside was a clean black lacquered wall panels with mother of pearl inlaid designs. They were very ornate facsimiles of what looked like ancient Egyptian hieroglyphs, but somehow different, I couldn't put my finger on it, but the symbols didn't quite look right.

The floor and ceiling of the elevator was solid cedar wood and the smell was an invigorating aphrodisiac for some reason. I was in awe, being taken back a bit from the lavish life style I was catching a glimpse of; I was both sickened and intrigued. The mini water fountain and the beautiful harp music were proving successful in keeping my rapidly diversifying emotions in check. I thought to myself, this elevator and this situation with Candace felt so right, but equally wrong for so many reasons.

That was the first real connect that clicked to spark the moral question as to the means we use in acquiring goods or knowledge and the motivation for desires and our own justifications we ultimately comfort ourselves with at night. I remember drifting, lost in that moment in the elevator. When we reached the top, the doors opened to reveal an immaculately ornate corridor leading to a very tall set of doors.

The ceilings of the corridor were at least 20 feet high, the door not much less than that. The walls were decorated in what looked like thousands of small carvings in majestic detail and everything was bright white, made even brighter by the late day sun shining through the spanning glass sky lights that stretched to the doors. There were security personnel there also, one at either end of the corridor. This seemed strange to me since after entering, found there was no one else home at the time.

I was impressed by the cars and the elevator, but really had no idea what I was talking about until I entered the foyer and had to almost have my jaw lifted off the ground. It was the most absurdly grotesque display of wealth I had ever seen, simply put, hands down. It literally looked like the scenes from movies depicting Zeus's palace on Mount Olympia. Massive marble pillars soaring upwards of 50 feet to the Sistine-like ceilings.

"Make yourself at home, I'll just be a few minutes."

Candace went in the other room to get the coffee while I looked around. Top quality marble with beautifully complex veins of various colored minerals flared like distant galaxies through the marble walls; it seemed like the primary building material throughout most of the house, although there were many other examples of rare and unique materials used in very creative and odd ways, like the bathroom floors which were covered with precisely polished and heated magnetite stonework, the couch blankets and pillows made entirely of large white feathers and the vast store of precious stones and metals used which only served to spite common sense from my point of view.

I almost didn't notice Candace getting embarrassed while I was getting lost in this extreme vanity; she was anxious when she returned from the other room with our coffees. She walked over to where I was inspecting some of the statues around the perimeter of the great room and graciously offered me my coffee in a neat little white ceramic cup and saucer. It was hot but not undrinkable and reasonably flavored, just a hint of Irish Cream. I was very happy the way she just gave it to me, no third degree about how I take my coffee. The bold aroma of the French roast was overshadowed by the refreshing scent of common sense.

She spent a few minutes explaining what a few of the art pieces around the room were as well as when and where they were from. Conrad was extravagant collector of power-centric historical artifacts who definitely had a distinct taste, both archaic and arcane. There was definitely a theme of antiquity, but the artifacts didn't look related, but there felt like an underlying connection between them.

The almost reckless way these rare artifacts were displayed initially impressed me that they could just be replicas, but Candace assured me they were 100% authentic as I reached to pick up a nearby Viking warrior helmet. We day dreamed together about what it would have been like for the different people that owned these things there and what they had seen and where they'd been.

She noticed again that I was very enthusiastic about the artifacts and we had an excellent rapport going about ancient cultures. She caught me off guard when she took me by the hand as if to lead me into a private back room, which she was, just not hers and not for *that*. She led me up to the top level of the house which was where the bedrooms and living areas were, through another foyer and into her parent's bedroom.

There was a golden spiral staircase which wrapped around most of the room and led up into the very top of the skyscraper where the penthouse loft perched, this seemed oddly symbolic because it was definitely a custom staircase; it grew incrementally smaller toward the top. This was a physical representation of Phi, the golden ratio. Candace mentioned that the golden railing was covered in ancient Semitic characters all the way up; things were getting stranger by the minute. I asked

"so, what's the deal with all of this stuff, what does it mean to him?"

She shrugged and shook her head as she said

"he's been involved with some very shady people doing highly secretive things my whole life. He doesn't ever talk about any of it unless he's asked and even then, he just says he's an art collector which is clearly not true. He mocks what I do, yet his home is dripping with artifacts from the old world, he's a ridiculous hypocrite."

I gave her a sympathetic, but reserved smile. We began the ascent up the golden staircase up to a locked door at the top. Candace produced a key from the loose bun in her hair evocatively which subsequently caused her dark, soft hair to cascade down over her neck and shoulders. It had the intended effect on me which I'm sure she was hoping for, but I maintained my composure with the anticipation of what other interesting things she was going to show me.

She suavely opened the door and the directional track lighting came on over several very unique items, most encased in various ways to protect them. This was Conrad's personal and very private collection of his most prized relics, what I saw was even more surprising than what I'd seen downstairs already. Everything was perfectly lit and displayed and labeled with engraved name plates and a brief description.

There was a framed letter, hand written and signed from Adolf Hitler to Conrad's father, Augustus Vanderbilt. It was a personal thank you letter thanking him profusely for a very generous financial gift to the Third Reich. He had the fabled sword of Charlemagne's paladin Roland known as Durendal, apparently thought to have been lost or be encased in a French cliff in Rocamadour, Candace explained.

There was an original copy of the Declaration of Independence. There were ancient Sumerian and Egyptian statues and pieces depicting reptilian like figures and their old gods. There was a hooded Druidic robe and hanging next to it was a very disturbing bloodstained suit which was labeled "JFK" This was turning out to be a very sick and disturbing trophy room he was keeping, but

"why?"

was the burning question I thought to myself. There was a piece of shrapnel like metal that looked like it had been ripped off something much larger. It still appeared to have some kind of power although there were no wires or visible power source, but it was pulsing slowly with cold, pale green light which was emanating from all sides of the metal, the name plate read only one word: "Dropa."

There was a moon rock and right next to it, a similar sized one from Mars, both in front of a poster sized photo of the first moonwalk. The photo was taken with a wider field of vision so you could clearly see the iconic shot we all know of the astronauts standing next to the American flag on the moon, but this was an uncropped version on a set in a very large space surrounded by gaffer and lighting equipment, cameras and casually dressed men on the outskirts of the frame. There were royal jewels of past monarchs from around the world and many more examples of things he had no business having.

At the center and far side of the room was a pedestal that stood just above the waist with a platform further elevating its contents and encased in glass. This was the sole item that carried no descriptive nameplate on it. I asked Candace about this one as I slowly walked closer to it.

"What is this"

I said with a curious wonder.

"I'm not sure and honestly I don't think my father knows either, it's the only one without a name plate"

she laughed. She further explained that she got to see a lot of what he has in his collection as he acquired the pieces over the years, some she found out about later after she secured a copy of the key to this room a couple of years ago.

"He would kill me, and you if he knew anyone were in here. This is definitely off limits."

I walked around the case a few times as slow as I could while still moving, the bamboo flooring slightly creaking every couple steps, studying what it might be. Candace was opposite, but moving in sync with me, like a Mexican standoff, studying the enclosure... studying the tension.

What was inside was remarkable, even though I didn't know what it was. It looked like a floppy piece of skin, but nothing that would belong to any animal I'd ever seen. It was suspended on all of its oddly shaped corners by very small bungee cords with small clips on the ends, like a condenser microphone in a recording studio. It looked like it was slowly and fluidly wavering like a giant flag on a light breeze, but only slightly.

The base color was a light camel color like an old pirate map and covered in what looked like stars, constellations and galaxies in every color which seemed as integrated into the skin as freckles on a face are. There were strange patterned lines embedded like veins throughout it. I slowly and quietly asked Candace

"do you know anything about it at all?"

as I looked up toward her. She said

"I've only seen it a few times, I don't really come in here that often, but I've never seen it do that before."

she said with a slightly alerted and higher pitched tone of voice. I hadn't noticed a difference until she said that and looked back. It was amazing and we both watched stunned as the skin started moving with a little more vigor, increasing in speed as we watched frozen and speechless. After a couple of minutes, it was all but writhing in its tiny shackles, tenuous as it was.

It moved like an amoeba, but much more three dimensionally than the poorly animated grade school filmstrips. It appeared dry like a finely treated piece of expensive leather, but elastic like a bat's wing. Its motion was as fluid as an octopus and even more graceful. I bravely or maybe it was instinctively asked her

"can I touch it?"

I looked up at her and her eyes met mine and we both and we both busted out laughing and to which she quickly rebutted

"get your mind out of the gutter, so mine can get by"

with a devilishly innocent smile. Her multifaceted hair was caught in the overhead light that beamed down and contrasted her rich lips and fair skin for a moment. In hindsight, I am sure that when I placed her illuminated hair back behind her right ear, it was purely instinctual. Our eyes met briefly again and I held her gaze while she returned the same plus a hint of relief and assurance.

As if to bottle the moment, she excitedly looked back to show interest in the skin's erratic movements, then back to me as if she were waiting for me to unwrap a gift. I snapped out of it with a dorky smile and we both took a deep breath before I slowly reached toward the organism. Maybe it was the electricity and adrenaline I had just been feeling with Candace or just rattled nerves, I chickened out and yanked my hand back quickly taking another deep breath.

"Do you have a pen or something?"

I asked. She grabbed one off the adjacent desk and quickly had it in my hand, smiling with anticipation. It felt like Russian roulette. I reached over again to gently nudge it with the end of the pen and when I did, the skin reacted. It was totally unexpected, but the way it reacted didn't seem threatening, quite the opposite. It seemed like it was being excited by the contact, more specifically, like it was being tickled.

It acted intelligently like it wanted to be played with and was communicating this with its body language.

"Do you think I can hold it?"

I said, pausing for a moment

"or do you think it will let me I should say"

she whispered cautiously, but unhindered while covering her mouth with one of her delicate hands. I extended my hand again to touch it with the back of my index and middle fingers to test the waters a bit more. It immediately responded again, differently this time. It flattened out and began to shiver it seemed, vibrating and moving in small tight oscillations. I could also describe it like it was simmering, just about to come to a boil.

Simultaneously, the colored space scape design that was covering it started illuminating and rotating it's morphing, multicolor spectrum throughout the design on the skin. The strange circular vein lines seemed to be undulating. It was becoming increasingly animated in its color and actions.

We both looked to each other with open mouths in astonishment again. I reached back toward the skin, this time with both hands placing one hand behind it and the other in front, but not touching it yet. I looked to Candace who was already moving her hand to assist me. She began carefully unclipping the skin, starting at the lowest contact points and working equally upward on the side clips. When the last clip had released its frail prisoner it fell more slowly than gravity should have been acting on it, coming to a weightless rest in the palm of my hands.

It seemed dead now, as if we had just pulled it off its life support. The color was completely gone and the design was visibly fading, desaturated compared to its previously vivid tattoo-like lines and the camel colored base was turning paler too. I grasped the two top corners that were just released between my index fingers and thumbs and held it up in front of my face. Its tattered coastal edges formed the general shape of a wide letter "V" almost like an upside down pyramid, but with a rounded "u" shape missing from the base of the triangular skin.

"This doesn't look very good; do you think we killed it, whatever it was?"

Candace asked. I looked over to her almost grievingly about to respond when I suddenly was knocked back out of my current stance and struggling to compose myself. I felt my body lock up and felt paralyzed, but awake and aware to the highest degree. I find it difficult to articulate, even now. It felt like a massive funnel of light ended its concentration at the top of my head and a gapping energy connection to everything in the universe instantly opened up.

I heard Candace start to scream toward the end of this brief experience, but I was hearing and seeing everything happening in extreme slow motion. As soon as I started to hear her scream, I dropped to the floor from my immobile stance as I was not prepared to be *released* and landed with a hard thud on my left side. Candace's scream shifted into high gear when my head hit the bamboo floor and time returned to normal speed for me again.

Her hands shot to her mouth and she dropped to her knees hovering over me checking my vitals and trying to get me to respond. I glanced around looking lost and asked

"where's the skin?"

She looked at me horrified but still worried about my well-being. She was having trouble forming any words, on the verge of tears. She stuttered but couldn't say anything; she could only cross her hands and grasp her throat as if to motion to me. I didn't understand what she meant at first. She repeated her charade a couple more times and I reached for my throat and felt nothing unusual.

I also noticed that the scab behind my ear from the day before was now gone. When I did this, she got even more distraught and started crying profusely. The implant must have been forced out when I hit the floor. I found the micro-sized implant on the floor and inconspicuously pushed the foreign metal bit in between a natural curve of the wood flooring. I scooted closer to her as we were both sitting on the floor at this point in order to put my arm around her to comfort her. She quickly jerked away as if I had the plague now, she was genuinely frightened.

I looked at her confused because I was only trying to help console her and didn't understand what was happening. She was able to pull herself together with a visible muster of courage and hastily wiped the tears from her eyes.

"It's *in* you"

she muttered.

"When you were holding the skin up, it flew through the air and attached itself to your throat and sunk down into your chest, how could you not know that! The way it hit you… Didn't you see it? Didn't you feel it?"

I honestly had no idea that had happened and spent the next few seconds trying to convince her with my bewildered expression. It was true after all; I had no recollection of the event whatsoever.

"One second I was looking at the skin, the next I'm laid out on the floor."

I continued inspecting my neck and chest, feeling for anything at all, an edge, a bump, something, but it was like nothing ever happened. I asked her to look for me. I laid flat to give her good lighting and perspective to see if she could find anything. She looked me over for a few minutes and had nothing to report.

"Do you think it's still in me?"

I asked with a concerned look. I felt like it was a stupid, yet relevant question.

"I'm pretty sure we'll notice when and *if* it decides to leave you"

she said with blank-faced dry humor, clearly traumatized more than I was about what had just happened. I felt fine, in fact I felt great, better than I can ever remember feeling. There was an underlying feeling of energy that was moving all through me, it felt like a wave of electricity swishing around and through every cell in my body and I felt a strange new familiarity with everything around me.

My euphoria was short lived when we heard the front doors slamming from downstairs and the echoing of footsteps through the massive marble foyer, leaving no time to talk about what had just happened. Candace reacted quickly, putting the glass cover back on the pedestal, grabbing me by the hand and rushing quietly out the door, locking it behind her as the lights dimmed out.

We rushed down the golden staircase and out of the room and into her bedroom which was two rooms adjacent on the same level. We heard her father go into his room and shuffle a few things around. He was just grabbing a quick shower and getting changed before heading right back out again. We waited for a few minutes to get our wits about us and decide where we were going to go to get out of there to breathe easy.

Her father's shower was unexpectedly short. Conrad called out as we walked past his doorway when he noticed us heading down the stairs.

"Candace, can I get a hand"

holding out his arm fumbling with a cuff link that was barely hanging on to his right sleeve. She looked at me with disappointment toward him and silently mouthed an expletive and rolling her eyes before turning around to oblige his request. He seemed in good spirits and eager to meet me saying

"So who's your little friend there"

bobbing his head as if to get a better look at me. I was extremely nervous he would recognize me from the protest videos if Candace and so many others had seen it. I turned around and walked up the mere two stairs we had gotten down before he beckoned us. I walked over and said

"it's Asher sir, nice to meet you."

"Oh okay"

he politely replied.

"So what are you two up to?"

he said. Candace tersely replied

"just studying for a research paper I'm writing and Asher had some great insight on it."

"I see, about what?"

he was prying and I could tell it was making Candace slightly uncomfortable.

"It's about Scandinavian migration patterns over the past millennia"

she said proudly. He gave her a belittling half smile and walked out promptly after Candace finished helping him with his cufflinks. We followed him out of the room and down the stairs where he was already getting a bottle of sparkling water from the fridge. Candace said

"See you later"

and motioned for me to follow, to which he promptly responded.

"I'm leaving too, we'll ride together"

very matter-of-factly, he wasn't asking and Candace was not contesting it, so I just went with the flow. We all left together, down the elevator and into the waiting town car in the garage.

"Get a good look at my cars?"

Conrad asked.

"I'm just curious since Candace doesn't bring many people over."

"Yes they're very impressive"

I said, not really knowing where to take this. He didn't really show that he cared for any of our responses anyway, it felt more like a pseudo-friendly interrogation. A couple of minutes of silence passed before he asked

"So where are the two of you headed?"

to which Candace replied

"the library at Columbia, research never ends"

He motioned to the casually eavesdropping driver to give his approval of the destination. We arrived a little while later and Candace said

"Thank you father"

and they both smiled fake smiles to each other. Candace got out first and I followed suit, but just before I exited, he grabbed my upper arm tightly and pulled me closer. His fake smile flipped like a switch to dead serious and he whispered darkly to me

"How's the ear Asher?"

He let go right away as to not raise the suspicion of Candace and switched back to his sinister P.R. smile. I shut the door and Conrad rolled down the back window to say

"Have a good time you two... stay out of trouble"

He was still smiling and waving goodbye. It was very surreal, creepy, but most importantly, enlightening. My synapse started firing intensely with the possible implications of what just happened. He knew exactly who I was and somehow knew something about my secret detention.

Ch. 3
| victory |

I followed Candace into the science library where she stood, still waiting for me. We both looked over at each other, smiled and walked out.

"I would kill for some Chinese"
she said.

"I'm starving, we could do take out at my place, it's not too far from here."
I replied. We took a cab. Back at my drafty shell of a home, we found our dinner table made out of a nest of what blankets and pillows I had lying around. It wasn't five-star, but it felt like it. We talked about cooking methods, gourmet ingredients and she told me about trips she had been on all over the world and the different kinds of food she'd had there. It was really cool to hear her take on the way certain dishes we eat in America had been adapted and were made totally different in their actual country of origin and how she preferred the Americanized version of some and the authentic version of others.

We quoted random movie lines all night trying to see if we could stump each other; it was a pleasant surprise to find we were well matched in this geekery. We had glutinous amounts of boxed red wine and dark chocolate that we gorged on before falling asleep to silent movies. We woke up in the same position we fell asleep in, I was behind her, our arms and legs intertwined like grapevines. Every sunrise still takes me back there.

"I had the most amazing dream"

I whispered.

"Me too"

she said with a smile as she rolled over to face me. I followed closely with

"but I can't remember it."

She kissed my nose which turned my confused countenance to a sudden smile and a quick, but hard kiss on her lips. I got up to throw a pot of coffee on and get myself together. I quarantined myself in the bathroom to get cleaned up. I looked at my hair and put on a hat and began gargling to nix the morning breath. I couldn't tell if it was in my head or outside, but there was a deep rumbling sound that seemed to correspond with the time I was gargling and humming.

I thought I had and ear infection or slept on it weird maybe. I cautiously tested this anomaly further, humming the star spangled banner, very slowly and deeply, but quietly. I felt the aether around me quiver with responsiveness. It was completely mind bending. I was ecstatic but nearly paralyzed with fear. What and how was this happening?

All I could think was *hopefully* that starskin had positive or at least symbiotic intentions when it sank inside me.

I desperately needed to know *what* it was because as exciting as it was, my adrenaline was fueling my terror. I could see everywhere, what looked and felt like ripples on the surface of calm water when you drop a pebble in. I felt a distinctly heightened sense of awareness with all my senses, that awareness was a sixth sense, like waking up for the first time. I could feel this endless energy flowing through my body; I could feel it well up inside me when I focused on intense feelings or concentrated on it.

I could feel a noticeable improvement in the way I could control this sensation with every time I practiced harnessing it and feeling it out. I decided to do a little experiment and went back to our nest that Candace was still lounging in half asleep. I knelt down close to her and she smiled but kept her eyes closed.

"Keep your eyes closed, tell me if you feel this"

I hovered my hands over her curled up body, closed my eyes too and concentrated all the positive thought, love, good intensions and light I could possibly envision on her. I visualized it coming from a source above me into the top of my head, rushing through my body (which I could actually feel and was intensely experiencing) and not only exiting through me, but when I was near her, I could feel this energy quickly becoming reciprocal, passing through both of us now.

This was definitely different than what I felt in the bathroom earlier. It climaxed to a point that I couldn't physically take any more and had to divert my thought to break this ethereal link between us that felt like it was going to implode us both. I opened my eyes to find her uncontrollably weeping, so deeply that she couldn't make a sound. The pillow she lie on was soaked with tears. I almost panicked inside, not knowing what I had done.

"Oh no, are you ok, I'm so sorry, what's wrong, where are you hurt?"

she attempted a smile to try to reassure me but what had her was too intense to break away from. She shook her head and her body language told me to just give her a minute. I held her in the silent, cold room watching the dust particles move through the square morning light beaming on to the concrete wall.

I was worried about her and that emotion was blocking any kind of intense positivity I was trying to concentrate on her, but this worry was subsiding the longer we laid there together. Feelings of extreme contentment were beginning to overtake the worry and that same intense feeling between us started welling up again. I know that she felt it because it was at that point when I noticed that she was feeling it start again too.

"That! That's what was happening earlier... what's going on Asher?"

"I'm not sure. I don't think it's a bad thing, but I'm sure it has something to do with that skin that's in me now. Where did you say it's from again, I don't think I heard you say before"

I said.

"I didn't say... all I know is that he brought it home from a business trip about ten years ago, he's never talked to me about it, I don't even think he knows I know what's in that room. I'm really worried about what he's going to think or do when he finds out it's gone. He's going to just lose it."

She had such a soft spoken tone that it was hard to feel any fear from that.

"Don't worry, it'll be ok. There's no way he could prove it was you"

I tried to assure her.

"You don't know my father, he's totally paranoid. There are cameras pretty much everywhere he goes and in everything he owns. They are all over our house and it's only a matter of time before he finds out it was us that had last been around before it went missing."

She didn't really look as worried as she should be based on what she was telling me and I was hoping that it wasn't because of misplaced faith in me. I was certainly no match for a man with Conrad's money and power. I thought now was a good time to let Candace know what happened in the car the day before. I told her what he said to me as I was getting out of the car. I told her what happened to me for those two weeks I had "disappeared" and what happened to my equipment and other belongings in my apartment.

I put it all on the table knowing full well that she may call me a liar and never want to see me again. Her calm demeanor took a turn toward frantic and there was real fear in her eyes.

"We have to leave, right now!"

she said uncharacteristically loud. She stood up and started gathering her things.

"Get anything you're going to need for a while, seriously, let's go, we'll talk on the way"

she stressed. I made the rounds in the shell of a home I was saying goodbye to in less than sixty seconds, grabbing only a few essentials and we were out the door, down the stairs and down the street. We both opted for sunglasses as we tried to garner as much space between us and our latest haunt. After a few blocks we started conversing about the gravity of the situation and what to do next. This was a new level of helplessness.

Conrad Vanderbilt owned hundreds of properties in the city, it seemed like everywhere we thought to go would be a risk. We just kept walking and talking, jumping from crowd to crowd to camouflage ourselves. We were getting a little paranoid at this point although we had not seen anything or anyone to alarm us; we were on edge and alert. We decided to duck down into the 59th street subway entrance at Columbus Circle to regroup ourselves.

The urban cave boasted antique green décor, stained streaks on the walls, liquid dripping from the crusty ceilings and the platforms were dangerously cluttered with temporary structures. I always found that odd that things would be worked on for so long with so little accomplished, but I always just chalked it up to bureaucracy, especially with the city. We both shared the end section of the old bench protruding from the wall, not ten feet from a very old looking wood door covered in cracked paint and a blue informational sign.

I put my arm around her and she immediately sunk into me resting her head on my shoulder; we were both mentally drained and tired from the jog. We sat there in our own silence not engaged in people watching or eavesdropping at all. We both started to almost doze off in our own world and with my first nod off I snapped myself to attention and stood up to pace a little to get the blood flowing, Candace was still dozy and tipped her head back and continued to close her eyes after seeing I was just pacing. I did this a few times, not paying attention to much of anything outside of my mind.

I did an about face in front of Candace and started back to the subway stairs and did another one-eighty. I felt the hairs on my spine stand up as I turned. On the way back toward her, my eyes were averted from the silent conversation I was holding with the dirty platform floor to the snaking handle to her purse that was sitting on the floor where her feet used to be, she was gone without a sound.

Ironically, I got tunnel vision as everything around me faded to a black surrounding vignette. In a panic, I roughly asked the old woman who had been sitting next to us on an adjacent bench if she had seen anything.

"No, I didn't see anything"

was her only response. I rushed over to another guy standing close to the edge of the platform

"No, sorry man"

was all I got from him. There were a few other people leaving and coming in other than that. I would have seen her leave through the only public exit and I would have heard her run across the platform if for some insane reason she ran across, jumped off and headed down the tunnel. The whole room felt colder now and I found myself feeling a very discordant feeling that was making me very uneasy now. The only other door I saw there was the old one we were sitting next to, I tried opening it but it was locked and looked like it hadn't been opened for years. The blue sign with white lettering gave no indication of what was behind the door and there was no light on the other side from the cracks under and around its decrepit frame.

I kicked the door as hard as I could and pounded on it as I yelled like a primate out of frustration, only to get a face full of white dust when I did. I could still feel her like she was next to me, but I was drawing a blank in my current mindset.

"Did *anyone* see *anything*?"

I screamed out with only a resounding echo responding. Everyone just looked at me for a second then looked away, back to whatever they were doing. I sat where she had been sitting for the next hour or so before departing with my head hung low and not knowing where to go.

My eyes were pained from the break of daylight that hit my face again upon exiting the subway. I looked both ways down the street when I reached the top of the underground stairs and both seemed equally pointless now. I could still feel her but she was gone. All I knew was that I needed to find her, at any cost. I decided to keep heading toward uncovered ground, still very wary of the danger I was in.

I kept moving, stopping only for a minute at a street vendor to grab a hotdog and soda. I felt bad spending Candace's credits, but it was all I had and I was starving. I walked for a little while longer and decided to get on the subway at 33rd street. I was headed downtown, but not quite sure why yet. I ended up getting off at Fulton on William St. and started walking around again.

I heard sounds of a large crowd not far off and proceeded with extreme caution trying to locate exactly where it was coming from. I had a lot of time to think today at what had happened, that provoked a lot more questions than it did answers though.

"What was this"

I thought to myself.

"What was happening to me and what was this fugitive lifestyle all the sudden?"

I had come to the conclusion that if I was going to do anything, I was going to go all the way. I still felt the sting of Candace's absence, but also felt comfort in the fact that I could still feel her presence next to me and knew she was unharmed, for the moment. The more I thought about her the more clear her presence and thoughts became to me.

I began to see the ripples I had seen earlier that day. They seemed to be a kind of trail weaving off as far as I could see in front of me, coexisting around, through and with everyday materials like brick, signs & cars. The trails looked like thin, transparent highways with countless little ripples all along the otherwise invisible backbone, vibrant with boundless energy. They didn't seem to be affected by anything, but then again this was new to me and I was the only one seeing them apparently.

I'm pretty sure people thought I was either crazy or on some very hard drugs because I was slinking around and crouched down, looking out from behind a large street mail box. I was temporarily distracted by these ripple streams I was seeing while simultaneously still subconsciously aware of being spotted by the wrong people. This wasn't paranoia anymore, Candace had been taken and this was personal now.

Cowering behind a mail box was not decisive action. I stood up, got my wits about me and continued walking to try to blend in. I thought about how horrible of a spy I would be, this was not exactly my forte. I made my way a little closer to the crowd noise I had heard earlier walking down William Street. Thousands of people were gathered at the base of the Federal reserve building and were right in the middle of a very heated protest, much like countless other wall street protests had been increasing in popularity over the past few decades.

Protests like this and grassroots movements had almost become a hobby of the people of the world over the past several years especially and this was a big one. There were tons of people, a heavy police and SWAT presence, dogs, fire trucks, ambulances, and the National Guard was even mobilized with their specialized training and equipment. They had LRAD sound cannons setup around the perimeter and were in full riot gear.

They looked like they were ready for war, not keeping the peace. The handful of tracking drones overhead definitely did not put anyone at ease. There were megaphones being passed around the crowd. They would pop up when someone had something to say and disappear under the heads of the crowd when an officer would get close to them. Megaphones were banned in this area of the city and were only a misdemeanor, but an arrestable offense nonetheless. The crowd was playing keep away from them so they could keep their voices heard.

I was amused by this, only a lot. The police, not so much. They were getting frustrated with the crowd and starting to show their agitation by getting slightly more aggressive and getting into strategic positions. I moved closer to the outskirts of the gathering and slowly made my way inward. People were starting to recognize me and my noticing this felt like the event horizon, no turning back now. I kept moving slowly, but steadily toward the center of the crowd, smiling and obliging everyone who was noticing my temporarily relevant celebrity. It wasn't really fanfare, more of just whispers, saying my name, waving, etc.

We were listening to only relatively short bursts of protesting outcries from people in the effort to keep the bull horns moving through the crowd to whoever wanted to voice their opinion. All I could think about was Candace. The cocktail of emotion that was welling up in me felt like it was about to physically overflow, I couldn't describe it any other way. I knew I should say something and I wanted to chime in, but nothing specific came to mind.

The horns continued to be passed around and people's thoughts verbalized. People were talking about how awful inflation had become and how wages had stayed the same. They talked about the huge repercussions that stimulus payouts and bank bailouts from the last decade that had completely destroyed any chance of the American dream for most people.

They talked about the exponentially expanding abyss between the rich and the poor, the death of the middle class. There was no doubt that the people there were emotionally vested. The officers and the ones who sent them to babysit the crowd knew it and they knew that was the most dangerous opponent since they already had little left to lose.

Over all the chanting and megaphones from the crowd, a massive loudspeaker rang out

"This is an unlawful assembly taking place on private property. By executive order of the mayor of New York City, you are hereby ordered to immediately cease and desist or risk authorized use of physical deterrents including high-pressure water, sonic canons and tear gas. Disperse immediately. You have five minutes before this will be enforced. I repeat, disperse immediately, you have less than five minutes"

Very few people heeded this warning and departed, in fact, it seemed to be egging most of them on. The megaphones got louder and more frequent, people were starting to get really fired up and anything one person said was fodder for the crowd and fuelled the next verbal assault from the nomadic megaphones. Someone near me called out

"In 2002, I graduated with a degree in computer science, in 2005, I was a home owner, in 2008 I was laid off and foreclosed on and my wife left me shortly after that, since then, I have been unemployed or underemployed and 28 years later, my mailing address is the 30th Street shelter. How's that for an American Dream?"

I gave him a stoic, but empathetic nod and he extended the megaphone over my way and my body flooded with bi-polar emotions. I paused for a moment to look around at all the individual faces in the crowd now starting to avert their attention toward me. I slowly raised the device, the contrast of my soft spoken tone sounded out of place amplified.

"Three weeks ago, I was just a college student with a part time job, 2 weeks ago as some of you may remember, I was at the protest for the acquittal of NanoCell CEO Conrad Vanderbilt, after which I was unlawfully arrested and secretly detained for two weeks for exercising my first amendment rights."

There was a huge cheering uproar from the crowd that I could feel throughout my body, I could actually feel their energy coursing through my veins and soul, it felt as if the energy might lift me off the ground at any moment, it was a very surreal sensation.

"I was kept in a cage, tagged with a tracking implant like a test animal and apparently released due to public pressure from good people like you, to whom I feel indebted to, so thank you!"

There was a contrasting verbalization from the crowd after this, befuddled and very discontented boos and a lull of viral conjecture spread through them. I paused for just a moment to hear and feel them.

"During that time, my apartment was broken into, all of my research, equipment and anything I valued was taken by men in unmarked uniforms, without a warrant. Earlier today, my dear friend Candace, the daughter of Conrad Vanderbilt has now been taken by an unknown group or individual, literally when my back was turned and if I'm next, I'm right here for you to see. I will not cower and hide."

There was an overwhelming response from the crowd who erupted like the earth opening up and just then a voice resounded over the police loud speakers

"disperse now, you have been sufficiently warned and the grace period is now over, I repeat, disperse now!"

They gave about five seconds before flipping on several fire hoses on the crowd, this proved to have little impact on the solidarity of the moment and most everyone stayed in place. They quickly switched to their LRAD sonic canons which had an immediate crippling reaction to everyone. I felt an intense burning sensation rush through me after about a second of the noise pollution which instantly filled my body and just as soon, burst out of me as screamed a drawn out

"No!"

It felt like the burning sensation was exorcized from me like a demon and resounded with an ultra-wide frequency drone sound that made the ground beneath us tremble, the windows from all the surrounding buildings shatter out and rain down tiny beads of broken glass around their perimeters and cut power to anything electronic for as far as I could see down the street. It sounded like a monolithic low roar combined with a shrill, electronic glimmering sound like the high pitch of a whirling motor. After the sound of raining glass had subsided, the whole area was completely silent for the longest five seconds of my life.

I was just as shocked as everyone who was now staring at me with their mouths agape in awe of what had just happened; it was the calm before the storm. I looked around and was very relieved to see that no one was hurt from the massive sound. The silence quickly crescendoed from nothing into a tidal wave of chaotic noise and movement.

It was interesting discovering the beginnings of the true power behind whatever this starskin inside me held while simultaneously sharing that moment with the world. People were now rioting with such maniacal intensity on their faces that I feared for my life in the center of this perfect storm that had just reared its ugly head again. I didn't quite understand what had happened myself.

There was little time to think. I instinctively resolved to get out of this mess and headed straight outward toward the perimeter that was quickly blurring by the moment. I managed to only get hit by a shoe of all things, a far lesser pain than I saw people enduring on my way out. I could only see a limited amount of what was going on around me as I struggled to keep my head covered to escape to safety.

I felt I was almost in the clear as I made my way out of the main mass of people and was rounding the corner of a large delivery truck when I was attacked by three men in black BDU's, two of them securing my arms with an iron grip as they zip-tied my hands behind my back and the third clearly their superior, although they wore no markings just like the ones who had arrested me before. I came to find out later that they were part of specialized task force, a black-ops project funded by the department of energy known as BlackCorp. and they answered to only one man, Conrad Vanderbilt.

He told me this himself less than an hour later as I awoke in the same detention facility I had found myself in a few days prior. It was a uniquely unpleasant wake-up call as I wiped Conrad's spit from my face and finding him towering over my waking frame. I tried to stand up but was slammed into the side of the cage when one of the guards pulled leash that was attached to the collar that had been placed around my neck like a dog, unbeknownst to me during my unconsciousness.

Conrad crouched down to my level, his feet still in the same spot as he was standing so he was balancing on the balls of his feet.

"Where is it?"

he said in a very serious, slow and cold voice; he was almost whispering. Again,

"Where is it?"

this time he yelled it at the top of his lungs, his veins protruding from his face and neck as he turned red with anger. This was truly a Dr. Jekyll and Mr. Hyde scenario displaying a man on the edge who was not used to being in a position where he wanted something he couldn't have. His psychotic tantrum and threats continued incoherently for a few minutes before he spat on me again, frustrated by my silence.

"See you in D.C."

he said with a sinister, but collected tone before turning to make a swift exit through the large metal doors at the end of the hall. As soon as the door slammed shut, the guard that had just yanked my face against the metal mesh walls was opening my cage door and gesturing me to exit at gun point, they did not saying anything and were not mincing words with their body language.

I pulled the leash through the mesh and exited the cage. Like before, one guard was by my side leading and the other by-standing guard heading up the rear with his laser-sighted assault rifle firmly planted in my spine this time. They led me to the same room with the colored doors, but I was not taken though the same yellow door, this time I was led through the red door.

It opened up into the same kind of platform where a single seated transport was waiting with an open door. This was a smaller transport than the one I was in before and this one had a hatch type door where the whole nose of the transport opened up to reveal its true nature. It was outfitted with a locking five-point harness and a locking collar.

My dog collar was removed and I sat down in the transport while one guard locked me down in the various restraints and the other with his gun's laser sight focused squarely between my eyes. They were making sure that I arrived at my intended location without incident and the way I was locked down, I didn't doubt their ability to make this happen. My mind was racing, but I remained calm as I wasn't in any position to resist at this point.

He triple checked all the restraint points and shot me a nasty glare. He was inches away from my face at this point, starring me down. He thought it would be funny to punch me in the stomach since he had a wide open sucker punch opportunity and didn't seem to particularly like me for some reason, or maybe being a meathead left him with little choice. He just laughed with his douchey smile as he slammed the transport door down. He pushed a button on a nearby control panel and I was gone in a flash.

I was heading down a black tunnel at an amazing rate of speed, only the exterior lights of the transport lit the blurred wall that was rushing past the small windows. I was between a rock and a hard place, literally and figuratively speaking. The transport showed no signs of slowing; in fact it felt as if I was accelerating. I couldn't tell for sure, it was more of a sensation, but subtle. The micro-craft I was in was not on rails like a train, but felt very precise in its movements still while remaining almost silent, only a slightly fluctuating whirring sound could be heard.

I was in the transport no more than five minutes before I heard a massive, but faint plunging sound. I could only see for a split second, but it appeared that my path had been diverted from its original course as the transport shifted sharply downward, deeper underground; I saw my original path disappear behind me. I could tell I was headed straight down into the earth now because I was hanging from my multi-point harness at this point, dangling like a cherry on a branch over a garbage can.

I put my feet on the sides of the transport so I could have something to stand on to relieve the uncomfortable pressure of the harness points that were fairly uncomfortable now, but only for a moment. Very quickly I was pushed back in my sitting position, but not because the direction of the craft had shifted; I must have been going at least three times the speed I was going before the course diversion.

I was definitely sweating it at this point, eyes glued shut and teeth clinched so tight I thought they would shatter in my mouth. I couldn't breathe, like the wind had been knocked out of me, but it was only from the fear. This went on for only two or three minutes before I felt the craft start to decelerate and I felt the transition between g-forces holding me on my back and gravity taking over.

The craft started slowing more dramatically now and a small light appeared at the end of the tunnel; I found that very ironic when I saw it because I thought of how rare that kind of scenario must be to be able to use it literally, I laughed to myself to help calm my adrenaline.

Ch. 4
| beauty |

The light was getting brighter as the opening neared; it was much bigger than I surmised at first sight. It must have been about 25 feet in diameter. The light was bright enough now that I could clearly see that there were no tracks or anything that the transport I was in could be riding on. The walls of the tunnel were only dirt and rock, but it didn't look loose on the walls, they were hard and fairly smooth like an old dirt road.

I was a few hundred yards away when I could feel the warmth of the sun on my face. As I approached the tunnel's horizon, it started to curve more and level out and seconds later I had finally escaped the darkness of the tunnel and come to a gliding standstill in an open field of grass. It was long and softly moving in a delicate breeze. I looked around through all the windows of the shuttle and saw an amazingly foreign landscape I had never seen before.

I had no idea where I was and what I was seeing didn't make any sense at all. It didn't look much different than artist representations of the Mesozoic era I had seen in textbooks. Everything was massive and growing wild; I had never seen such lush greenery. It was foreign looking, but still somehow familiar. There were no latches or buttons or anything I could find to free myself from my constraints. I hoped this wouldn't be the way I went out. Disappointed, tired and disenfranchised, I relaxed to soak up the beautiful scenery at least. It looked like I was in one of many valleys as I could see other green rolling hills and peaks all around.

In the window above me, I realized that the sun didn't look right at all. It looked dimmer than it should be. I thought it was just clouds at first glance that was the cause of this, which turns out it was, however after a double take, I noticed that the clouds that were covering the sun were actually moving in beautiful random movements, rushing around and through each other, almost like snakes, but they were thick ribbons of clouds that seemed to have more mass and substance that a cloud. There were no breaks in the clouds where any beams of light shot out, it just emitted a constant warm light. The cloud cover over it was semi-translucent; it was clearly still letting light through, but didn't look like a storm cloud either, more of a smoky haze I suppose.

I was so preoccupied at trying to figure out what was going on with the sun that I didn't notice the creature standing in front of the craft, staring at me with cold black eyes. It wasn't doing anything threatening, it actually seemed peaceful and just observing me; I was both awestruck and frozen in terror. It was very tall and slender, wearing no clothing or adornments of any kind that I could see.

Its skin was gorgeous and infinitely intricate in its unpredictable patterns. Its skin was a dark clay color, an earth tone based hue basically and the texture was not unlike the palm or our hands, smooth, but with lines and unique characteristics throughout it. The skin seemed to be thicker than ours the way it folded around its body at certain points, but still thin, like a fine suede leather. The skin was tightly wrapped all around the humanoid frame of the creature still observing me as I continued to decipher my surroundings and keep my cool. The most amazing feature of this skin was that it was multi-colored in a way. The color was subtle and subdued; it seemed to almost shine above the base skin color. An oil slick on a puddle was the only thing that came to mind as I was watching it, watching me.

All this was running though my head in a matter of seconds. The creature extended its long fingered hand upward, similar to the position someone takes when taking an oath. Suddenly, the transport door sighed open and my constraints literally fell open; all of the points on the seatbelt harness and the lock around my neck were completely loose and hanging flaccid now. I looked down and looked back at the creature before me a couple of times. This was obviously something the creature had done, but

"how?"

I thought to myself, unable or unwilling to speak. It was for the best and did not matter because at that moment, I heard it speak to me and felt it speak to me. Its mouth did not move and I did not hear with my ears. The voice was not hollow with a cave-like echo like you see in the movies, it was inside of my mind and body and was more clear than my own thought, in fact, it drowned out my own inner monolog, thoughts and most importantly for me, my fears were rapidly conceding as I felt this powerful connected focus on my mind.

The sun seemed even warmer now and I felt completely at ease in a matter of moments although I still did not know much more than I did a few moments earlier. I was being calmed by the creature. The voice said

"Welcome Asher, I am Nelis; rest your fears, you are safe. You are known to us and your arrival is by our will for a great purpose."

I could hear this, but more interesting to me is the fact that I could actually feel what it was saying; the feeling was reinforcing the words to further confirm its meaning to me. It was eerie, but strangely comforting. The communication felt very direct and focused at me, but I could feel it coursing all through my body like soft waves. I felt a magnetic connection to objects around me as I felt certain words like a fluid sequential rhythm drawing me to my physical surroundings as the words hit me and washed through me.

When I felt my name, I felt a strong connection to everything outside of me rushing in and everything inside me rushing out simultaneously as if there were no more borders between my body and the world around me. When I felt the word "love", there was a direct pulling feeling to the sun above me, I could feel its warmth increase. The word "will" caused a pulling toward Nelis and I could hear and feel its heartbeat, the word "great" connected me to the nearby lake and could smell its purity and could even hear air bubbles scintillating through the water.

I could feel a strong sensation rousing all of my senses, and in different ways with certain words, it was very confusing and overwhelming at first having all of my senses fire at once. Some senses were more dominant with certain words, but even the more dormant senses were heightened to a level I'd never experienced before. I was very taken by this moment and still trying to process the reality of what was happening to me as I paused for what felt like forever, but what was really only a few seconds before Nelis *spoke* again, this time "syncing" his thoughts with my mind telepathically.

"Please, walk with me"

with an outstretched hand as if to beckon to me and put an arm around my shoulder, but never touching me. Almost in a trance from what I was feeling and seeing, I began walking through the wide open field of grass which went on for miles around us in every direction. The grass was not rough on the edges like most tall, overgrown weeds. It felt very soft like feathers almost and each step we took released a sweet herbal smell that filled my whole head with a cleansing warm spice, washing away any residual anxiety I had previously felt.

I began hearing and feeling subtle sounds throughout my body and mind here and there, but I could not make anything out as a distinct word or sound I was familiar with. They definitely had a musical tonality and sweet harmonic feeling to them, but they were faint and just whispers on the wind.

As we walked, there was no shortage of strange and beautiful creatures and scenery around me, most of unusually large size. Everything seemed somewhat familiar, but eccentric exaggerations of things I knew, like birds with what looked like three tiers of tail feathers and an additional ridge of wings extending further forward and outward past a normal set of wings and adorned in bright royal toned feathers that billowed over their large bodies like fluffy feather boas.

I saw what seemed to be large ray-like creatures sitting on top of the water of the adjacent lake like giant lily pads. I only noticed them when their massive flat and round bodies would lift up the edge in an oscillating motion that would round their entire bodies like the circular scraping motion when you dislodge the edge of an egg stuck to the sides of an omelet pan. I can only assume they were repositioning themselves on the surface of the water as dozens of them were sunning themselves.

There wasn't any more communication from Nelis other than a calm demeanor and the subtlest of smiles which seemed to be gratification in my fascination. I only felt brave enough to glance over a couple of times to notice this, not out of fear really, more that I felt slightly awkward in knowing how to approach anything.

We had only been walking a short while when all around me I felt a change in my physical surroundings, starting first with a sort of tingling feeling in my body like when I felt my name earlier then a slipping sensation and my soul or inner being stretch out and forward while my physical body continues walking normally. Even though I could not feel a physical difference in my stride, inside of me felt similar to when you step off a moving sidewalk at the airport or an elevator moving.

I was feeling this change inside myself while simultaneously seeing the scenery around me blur like I was walking into a different dimension. I felt my chest and face in a panic as if to prove to my physical hands that what they were feeling was real and all this was based in reality still. Everything around me looked different. It felt like the same place but now I was high on a hillside facing a massive structure that looked as though it was growing out of the earth that surrounded it. I looked behind me and far off in the distance I could see the lake and the field I had just been walking through moments before. I turned back quickly to take in my new surroundings.

The great building looked like it was constructed of dark slate colored rock that towered several stories high, but not like an office building with multiple levels. There were only three levels that I could see, but each level must have been 50 feet high. There were huge hexagonal pillars of this stone all over supporting the building, but the construction seemed so organic and imperfect, I wondered how it could be supporting a building so large.

It was perfect enough to form beautiful architecture unlike any I had ever seen. It looked kind of like an old world Greek building or temple and kind of like a castle and all over its slate exterior was the lushest foliage I had ever seen. The deepest tones of every shade of green sprawled all over it. Ancient moss and ivy plants were most dominant, but were accented by gorgeous blooms of strange plants on ledges and in nooks in every imaginable color, including iridescent and luminous plant life I had never seen or imagined.

Taking in the beauty of this masterpiece almost took my breath away, what brought me back to my mind was the harmonic sounds I was hearing faintly earlier which had grown into a softly divine frenzy like the tremolo and trills of a symphony fading in and out of each other. It was a building, yet positive tension in the air around us. I felt warmth and love all around and through me. The sounds were passing through me as easily as my hand through the air and filling me with so much emotion that my whole body dropped to the ground, almost as if I were hugging it.

I was completely overwhelmed in this place, the heightening of my senses and the sounds of these perfect harmonies rushing through me. I just laid there for a few minutes, my face pressed against the warm, soft soil with tears streaming into the earth. I rose to my feet to find I was alone now. I hadn't noticed Nelis leaving, but I didn't have a chance to wonder what would happen next.

I was being approached by a beautiful woman slowly exiting the huge building and walking down the many slate steps toward me. She was dressed in a white flowing dress that seemed to not only be moving with her ask she walked, but actually flowing and moving in place on her skin the way loose fabric moves under water, slow, fluid and elegant. She was emanating a soft, iridescent white light from her skin; it was subtle, but unmistakable. As she got closer, I could see she was not like Nelis at all, she looked human, for the most part. She was shockingly beautiful; I found myself almost completed paralyzed by her.

She had a very fit physique, about the size of a teenage girl and white slicked back hair that extended most of the way down her back. She had slightly exaggerated facial features. Her striking eyes were such a light ice blue that they almost looked white. They were slightly larger and angled slightly upward. Her nose, mouth and ears were very streamlined and slightly smaller than normal, yet very human still. She had a very meek and innocent countenance, but was radiating such brilliance from her radiant white skin that she exuded extreme grace and confidence.

"Asher"

She spoke in a soft, yet concise tone.

"I've been expecting you"

she said with a slightly drawn smile as she extended her delicate hand out to mine. I reluctantly reached out as if to shake her hand and when our hands met she immediately synced telepathically to me like Nelis.

"Hold my hand as we walk. Here we are all one and there is nothing to fear because there is nothing to hide. We are all synced and this is how we prefer to communicate, if it pleases you?"

she turned to me still with her soft smile almost for a visual queue to confirm as a semantic pleasantry for my sake. I returned the smile and gave it a shot by just thinking to myself

"It does"

and I immediately heard a reply back from her syncing

"Good"

I was completely amazed and couldn't believe I had just communicated telepathically. My mind was racing a million miles a second and didn't know what to think, I heard her sync again

"Rest your mind, all things will be known" I felt what she said to be true as her words resonated through my body and gave me a calming reassurance.

We continued walking toward the building where she came from and up the stairs into a great open hall which was filled with plant life, like the exterior of the building. It was warm and slightly humid like a greenhouse and smelled like sweet flowers and fruit, almost to the point of a candy smell that reminded me of my childhood. There were also hints of cedar and juniper berries in the air mixing with the sweetness, combining to make an intoxicating scent.

We walked through the indoor gardens to the back of the foyer where we continued up a huge spiraling staircase up to the next level. At the top of the stairs was a long square corridor that ran the length of the building and led back to the front of the structure where we must have been standing directly above where the entrance was. I stopped in my tracks and looked up as she kept walking, breaking her hand away from mine.

I was standing there looking at a giant sphere that filled the entire cube-like space of the top two levels of the building. The sphere was translucent, but hazy with a glowing electrified look to it, like plasma was washing all over it in slow moving waves. The walls of the room were of the same slate grey rock as the rest of the building and there was nothing else in the room. It looked like a giant bubble. She stepped back slowly taking my hand again and we walked forward.

There was no irregularity in our calm stride as we walked seamlessly through its border, directly into the center of the great sphere. She motioned for me to sit, as she began, I followed suit in a simultaneous motion. We were both sitting in a flat kneeling fashion, facing each other with our knees almost touching and both our hands outstretched now and grasping the others'. I felt torn; I was incredibly uncomfortable and comfortable at the same time. Her glacier blue eyes were peering into me literally and I could not look away even for a moment, not that I wanted to, but at the same time I felt very exposed and unsure of what was happening. She began syncing her thoughts to me again

"My name is Vasha"

the sound of her voice was like a warm velvet breeze, blanketing my entire body.

"I am from your world but not of it. In my blood flows two great rivers, just as yours does."

"What do you mean?"

I asked.

"The female is the carrier, as she has always been; the fertile earth where a seed is sewn. You would not have been allowed to enter this world without the blood of your father. We are both from the same two worlds, but born the same world apart. We are the same Asher"

She had a stoic countenance while smiling within. It almost felt manipulative, but I came to understand it later as more of a multifaceted and complex communication rather than a manipulation. It was many entangled feelings at once.

"But I know my father and he is not one of them, or you"

I said. Sensing my doubt she replied

"You are not one with ordinary beginnings. Our mothers were known to the Atlantians and we are not unlike the Nephilim of ages past. Our differences are only that your mother was meant to keep and raise you on the surface so you would come to know the successes and failures of the human world; you were meant for a great purpose Asher. Do you really doubt that? After feeling different the way you've felt your entire life, after the experiences you've had and where you are sitting right now?"

She was right and put me at ease, at least for now. I closed my eyes and tried to clear my mind and picture myself on a calm morning water on a lake I visited as a child, a memory I commonly used to relax and reset the tension in my mind.

"Good"

Vasha said. I felt her close her eyes too and soon felt her forehead pressing softly against mine. When I felt the contact of our skin against each other I opened my eyes and found hers were closed, her face in a blissful focus and softly drawn smile again. A lightly fluttering electrical sensation which felt like what her dress and the patterned plasma waves of the sphere looked like, immediately ran from her skin all over me, quickly covering my whole body.

Her eyes still closed, I could not help but keep mine open in response to the strange wonders that were happening to me and my curious lack of understanding and disbelief of it all. This was more than a dream and more than reality, the best of both worlds. As our foreheads made contact and her sensation spread to me, her flowing dress that was previously full of life began to lose its fluid movement over her body and began a slow, poetic descent which soon surrendered to the floor around her exposing her perfect and pure form.

"Closer"

she synced to me. I unbuttoned my navy blue work shirt with my left hand. We both effortlessly slid down against each other's' bodies, coming to a rest opposite each other, our faces pointing downward with our left ears tuned to each other's fiercely beating hearts. Our hearts synced up to identically syncopated rhythms; it was the single most beautiful moment I had ever experienced. We both listened to the beating of our collective heart for what seemed like forever. When we opened our eyes and awoke to reality we noticed nothing that we felt, saw or touched was not shared by the other; our movements and being were synchronous.

We opened our eyes and found ourselves looking through each other's eyes down at the great lake I first stood beside when I arrived in inner earth, except there was no distance. Everything I could see, I could touch. I reached out and simply ran my finger through the cool waters and brushed my hand on the soft foliage that adorned the lakeside before pulling my hand back to rest at my side.

"I never grow tired of that smell. First, a clean grassy meadow until you rustle them, then it smells of warmly spiced honey"

Vasha said. It was warm now and there was a dreamlike comforting feeling surrounding and penetrating us. We were physically in the sphere and virtually anywhere on the ground, simultaneously existing in the same vantage point of the sun I saw when I first arrived. It was a surreal anomaly, not to mention I was still physically, emotionally and spiritually bonded as one with Vasha. We were one, as one.

"You're so beautiful and warm, I never want to leave"

I said with a new found confidence. There were no insecure barriers anymore, no awkward moments of insecurity. It was like talking to myself when I felt the best about myself, but at the same time being closer and more attracted to another person that I ever imagined possible.

"We are love and a single circle is complete"

she said. Her words melted and collapsed me completely in that instant. There was a harmonious frequency alignment that took us over and we continued from then on as a single duality, a phrase of perfection, sounding a divine pitch of unwavering, holistic unity. She smiled at me again and slowly averted her eyes from me down toward the inner earth still alive beneath us.

"Watch"

she whispered. I had to focus to move my eyes away from her calming countenance: as I looked down she ran her fingers through the lake just as I had done. As her thin fingers glided over and through the water a subsequent trail of fish followed piously after them and soon disappeared back under the water. She then rustled the leaves and grass on the lakeside and the foliage exploded with life as I watched a wide variety of creatures emerge as if they were urgently looking for something. They quickly disappeared into the plant life once again as she withdrew her hand.

I was amazed that I felt differently than I had before when I was doing the same thing. I understood her interpretation from her perspective and that was the difference. I could feel everything she was feeling as she did this. I felt the light and energy of the life below coursing through my body from hers in a reciprocating cycle. I felt the verbal names of the objects and smelled the fresh fragrances below as if I was there; everything was one and everything was present.

I felt a distinct lack of the sense of time around us which didn't feel as strange as I might have expected, in fact, it was like the subtle transient and unnoticed tension of life was suddenly relaxed and everything I could perceive flowed freely. Vasha's light was filling up inside her and she was smiling slightly more now after sensing my ray of enlightenment. She nodded her head slightly down as if to encourage me to try again.

I reached down slowly and as I did, we watched the water start to boil slightly which quickly increased intensity as I moved closer. As my index finger touched the water, the boil of the fish exploded into a leaping frenzy with fish of all kinds jumping up, over and around my hand; I could feel their cool sleek bodies tickling my skin as I withdrew it from the lake water. This time, she looked at me with wide eyes in amazement and gasped, clearly excited about what she saw happening.

"Asher"

was all she said and needed to say to reinforce this excitement. I reached back down and rested the back of my hand on the soft grass fields below. The size of my hand as I reached down seemed to stay in proportion to me, but was much larger than life, like a divine intervention.

As my hand came to a stop on the ground, it already had a massive amount of birds heading toward it and quickly began encircling my arm like a feathered tornado. On the ground, there was a simultaneous gathering of what was nearly a stampede of wild animals of every kind, including animals I had never seen, quickly converging on and around my hand and quickly began ascending up my arm. It felt ticklish at first but as I saw the great mass of animals growing larger watching them move closer to me like jack climbing the beanstalk.

The frenzy made me nervous as they kept climbing higher. As soon as I felt that urgency, the animals dispersed as quickly as they had come. I could feel that they were not running in fear, but instead responding to my feeling as if they were obeying them. I pulled my arm back and looked at it all over to be sure I hadn't brought anything up with me. I was relieved not to find any stowaways.

"Don't worry, they wouldn't be able to enter here with us."

Vasha said reassuringly.

"I have never felt such a draw. Your light is so radiant Asher."

I was amazed myself and felt completely energized by the experience.

"I'm happy you understand"

she synced to me instead this time. I found it endearing the way she was communicating to me in different ways. Vasha looked again toward the bottom of the sphere and reached down, but this time hesitating at the sphere's threshold for a moment, I felt her touch it which sent a magnetic swirling sensation through our bodies. We didn't experience this when we were simply passing through it.

It was as if the sphere sensed our intent and submitted to our will. Her palm lay flat on the base of the sphere for a moment before she swiped it to her left and we started moving. Everything I saw below was moving left to right; I expected the opposite reaction initially then realized through Vasha that we and the sphere were in fact the ones spinning and not the reverse.

She lifted her hand off the base of the sphere for a moment with the exception of her ring finger which she used to apply the slightest pressure the sphere to bring us to a smooth stop over a new location, just like a spinning globe. What I saw when I looked down was nothing short of breathtaking. I saw the earth, the surface that we are all familiar with.

I saw dark silhouettes with clear human outlines of people going about their daily lives; some silhouettes darker than others and some that looked blotchy with light spots. The darker shaded silhouettes were each accompanied by brilliant beings of light with an aura of light in the shape of a cat's iris in full daylight emanating around a hazy light human shape. I looked at Vasha and she synced to me

"This is what we really look like. We are always with you."

More amazing than this visual was what they were doing. The beings of light were actually turning the darker silhouettes lighter. The blotchy spots of light that were very small at first and slowly growing in size, they looked like monochrome thermal vision as I watched what looked like some kind of light transference from the light to dark beings. We watched them for a while and based on the increased movement, intensity and posture of the silhouettes, it seemed that the beings of light were actually healing the dark silhouettes.

There was a wide variety of the dark intensity of the silhouettes from totally black and every variance in between. There was not much grey color though, only a bit of grey surrounding the edges of the light blotches. Some of the beings became totally white from there darker state over time, but were still more of an ivory white compared to the beings of light. The other main difference was that even when the silhouettes became white again, they still did not possess the bright white aura that the beings of light did; they maintained the human silhouette lines.

Once they became white, the beings of light faded away and so did the silhouette; more would enter our field of vision as others would leave, but there was a distinctness of character for each, they did not seem faceless even though I could not see their faces.

"You've heard stories of guardian angels? These are they. They are always there, healing and protecting those that have the intent and the will to ascend themselves to a higher frequency"

Vasha synced. Watching this gave me feeling of warmth coursing down through my body like hot cider on a cold day, directly followed by an extreme welling up inside me that shot straight up my core through the top of my head. It was like a lightning bolt, hot, fast and electrified. The shot of energy leapt through the base of the sphere and into the realm we had been watching, immediately turning all of the dark silhouettes a remarkable pearly white. Like a camera flash, all of the silhouettes were whiter and brighter than the silhouettes that the beings of light had healed. They had a mother of pearl iridescence to them for the brief moment they were in view before disappearing.

I had felt sensations like that countless times before, even from early childhood when I would get excited, I could even do it at will if I concentrated a little; it was more like a muscle I could flex rather than an involuntary side effect of getting very excited or happy. I remember asking my mother what that feeling was when I was younger and got a watered down

"it's your happy place feelings"

answer. This time it *was* the result of me getting excited, but I immediately recognized the distinct welling up feeling and rode the wave of positive energy. It made me wonder just what had happened and what would happen if the feeling was not involuntary. For the first time since I'd come to this strange place, I felt a strong feeling of anxiety.

The connection between Vasha and I had gone from a warm, red feeling to a cold royal purple hue. It felt as if there was ice water flowing in my veins now. She looked at me almost in horror. I did not sense any anger, just extreme confusion and shock from her. There was still a bond that was clearly still connected between us, but there was a definite brief period where I felt her close off and felt no discernable emotion from her at all.

She took a moment to compose herself and process what she had just seen. She let go of my hand to raise both of her arms above her head to touch the tips of her ring fingers together and then lowering her outstretched arms to a rest at her side. As she did this motion, the sphere had disappeared around us completely by the time her arms came down.

"We must leave now"

she said. I could still feel our bond and could still sense her and feel her, but she chose to speak this time from what seemed to be a grave concern in her still voice. I felt the presence of our sync, but it was a cold silence. I stood up and reached my hand down to her to offer to help her up, but she just looked at me plainly as she rose herself, ignoring my gesture. Vasha turned away and began walking out of the great room toward the stairway and I unwittingly followed. I jogged for a second to catch up to her. I ran up ahead of her stopping at the top of the stairway and turned to face her

"hey, I'm sorry, I don't know what just happened, whatever I did, I didn't mean to…"

I said. "You have disrupted an ancient cycle and you will have to explain this. What has happened is known, they are waiting for us now" she said. I could hear both of our voices echoing in both the great rooms from our vantage point at the top of the stairs.

"They? They who?"

I said. I was showing my frustration at this point, but Vasha remained composed. She began syncing to me again.

"They who watch over us. They who watch over and protect this world, inside and out, and they are expecting us now Asher"

She moved past me quickly and assertively. I paused for a moment in concerned confusion before turning to follow her down the great staircase. I stared at the stairs and the fluid movements of Vasha's flowing dress gently moving down and over them, but never touching them.

I followed her through the lush courtyard and out the huge doors where we were met by two tall and imposing figures, not unlike Nelis. Our escorts were on either side of the doorway facing us as we exited the building. They turned and faced in our same moving direction walking in sync with us down the front stairs of the great building. We were directed past the side of the building down toward the south shoreline of the great lake.

We walked along a black sand beach with huge walls of dark stone on one side and the small rolling tide of the lake on the other. We followed the stretch of beach for nearly a mile.

Aside from the anxiety I felt, it was a pleasant walk and didn't seem that long. We came to the end of the stretch of beach and the end of the cliff wall that opposed the shoreline we had been walking.

It looked like the cliff wall jutted out into the lake like a peninsula where the beach ended if I was able to see it from a bird's eye view. There was nowhere else to go, yet we continued on toward the water and began walking *into* the water, I stopped just before the water. The other three were calf deep as they all stopped and only Vasha turned to look at me

"Asher, you must come, there is no choice in this matter"

she synced

"So, we're all just gonna go for a swim, or..?"

I said sarcastically. Just then I felt an invisible pull on my body, moving me forward until I was again in line with my party

"Don't fear Asher, no harm will come to you, this is the way"

Vasha synced. I felt an unexplainable trust with her but I didn't trust my own logic. I was an excellent swimmer, but all of that confidence washed away realizing the unrelenting hold that had a hold of me. It was as if I had lost all muscle control in my body.

The water was cool on my skin as it worked its way up my legs and up my torso.

Vasha looked over at me and smiled reassuringly just as I was taking a deep breath in before my face disappeared under the water.

I closed my eyes tight as a reflex, but was quickly curious when the cool sensation of the water and its movement over my body had disappeared. I opened my eyes and let out the giant exhale of air I was holding captive in my lungs in a huge sigh of relief.

We were all walking down the smooth descending slope of what looked like the same stretch of beach we were just walking on except there was a tunnel like structure of water around us. The water walls were not a glass type enclosure where you could just see that there was water surrounding us like an aquarium, the walls and curved ceiling were moving exactly like the waves on the top of the lake we were just walking past, as if the gravity was still on the opposite side of the water's surface. It was moving and lively, but carefully contained to allow us to walk through.

The feeling of the cool water was nothing more than a false sensation as I could clearly see we were all still completely dry. At the end of the long sloping tunnel we came to where the ground had become level again and we were met with a dead end wall of water. Our escorts did not slow and I still did not have much choice either. We continued walking directly through the wall of water. I flinched as I passed through and held my breath again, unsure of exactly what to expect. It looked just like walking into the surface of a lake if you could walk perpendicularly into it.

Again, we remained dry and entered into a room not unlike the giant sphere Vasha and I had just been in in the great building. We were completely alone now, our escorts did not appear on the other side of the water wall and the invisible hold over my body was gone now. This sphere was enormous, at least ten times the size of the one Vasha and I were just in.

We were completely alone in our silence. The only light and movement was a blue-tinted waving iridescence that was washing over the surfaces of the sphere, moving through each other and reflecting off each other in a curious way like ripples on a pond with a will of their own.

Ch. 5
| strength |

"How are you feeling today?"

the thin doctor said. The doctor with aptly fitting thin-wired glasses always asked the same questions, in the same order. I always met him with the same responses

"Nice weather we're having isn't it?"

he said. The sick irony of his first two questions was that I had lost count of how long I had been in this sterile, empty room. The only thing keeping me going was the thought of reuniting with Asher. I felt by now that it was going to be the last place I'd ever see. I felt my mind slipping further and further away from myself and every day was a struggle to retain my sane independent thoughts.

The room was almost a perfect cube shape, except for the slightly lower ceiling. It was completely white and was extremely well lit with no windows. The single door to the room did not have and handle and had a flush seal to the wall. I was given a TV dinner type of meal every 12 hours or so. It seemed like clockwork although I had no concept of time in this place.

I was given a plain white jumpsuit that closed with a single Velcro strip from the leg to the neck and otherwise naked. All of my clothing had been taken when I had awoken here, what felt like months ago. I was given a new jumpsuit and white plastic tub every week or so. The tub was the only thing I had to use as a bathroom as the room was completely empty otherwise. I usually sat or laid in the opposite corner when I wasn't pacing the room with my time.

The same thin doctor was the only contact I had with anyone or anything during my entire time there. At first I asked all kinds of questions.

"Why am I here? Who are you? What do you want?"

and a variety along those lines, but after a fairly short time, it became very clear that he was not going to answer any questions I had. He asked his third, predictable question as he crouched down to where I was sitting, balancing only on the balls of his feet

"Where is Asher Wry?"

I learned to follow suit in not answering any questions, since I felt like they were all being used to crack my sanity, especially this question since it was already eating at me. All I knew was that I ached for him and I was scared for him. I had gone over the scenario where I saw him last, just before I was taken. It seemed like a pointless waste of energy anymore since it didn't feel like I would ever leave this room.

When the thin doctor had heard enough silence, he slowly stood up and walked toward the door. It always buzzed with a raw industrial tone and lurched open slightly just as he neared it. He would open it further, pulling on the reverse side of the door. It would always close unprompted behind him with that same raw buzzing sound.

As awful and short as those mentally debilitating visits were, I almost looked forward to them in a sick way as it was my only human contact and my only real way of telling time besides the meals and clothes changes. I quickly learned to get over my shame of living this way since I had discovered the four tiny reflective lenses in each or the corners of the ceiling that I'm sure were cameras, always watching me. I felt like an animal and I was beginning to think like one more and more as time crept on.

I felt like I was nearing the ever-blurring edge of wherever my sanity met my primal instincts. I had thought many times about escaping but I was always too drained. I felt like I had a constant fog in my head, but I could focus on it clearly. It was if I could process everything that was happening to me, but couldn't connect the dots in my mind clearly. I had a clear sense that I was confused and early on, felt as if I was on pain killers or Nitrous Oxide at a dentist appointment.

My desire to escape was growing stronger every day, but I was always hesitant to try, not knowing what was on the other side of my white prison walls. I spent the next several hours really thinking through the patterns of the thin doctor and his routine visits. He would enter with the buzz of the door. As he stepped in the room, he would ask

"How are you feeling today?"

as his second foot entered the room and he would pause, as if to await my answer he knew he'd never get. He'd force a cold smile as he slowly walked over to me, his clipboard in his left hand and a pen in his right. As he walked he would ask his second rhetorical question

"Nice weather we're having isn't it?"

he paused more briefly after posing this one, acknowledging the triteness of it himself. Just before the third question, he would grab the fabric on the front of his pants and pull them up slightly with his thumb and forefingers and squat down coming to a balanced perch on the balls of his feet and ask his final question

"Where is Asher Wry?"

After my reliable silence, he would stand up and walk to the door as slowly as he had entered, the door would buzz and he would leave. I thought if I had any chance at all, this would be it.

I drifted off to sleep and had the first dreams that I can remember since being put here. They were vivid and fast and there were a lot of them, but I could only recall myself walking through a wall of fire as I shifted from dream state back into my cold reality as I was awoken by the sound of my meal hitting the floor from a small laundry type shoot that it shot through on its timed schedule. It was only a small enough opening for a large envelope to fit through, flush to the wall like the door.

I ate my bland food quickly as I always did, using only my fingers since I was never given any utensils. As the food settled hard on my aching stomach, I started getting excited as I thought about mustering the bravery to attempt an escape. I thought and waited, going over what I would do when the thin doctor came today. As thin as he was, I was no physical match for him in my weakened state and knew I only had one chance if I was going to pull anything off successfully.

I sat in silent thought until I heard the buzz of the door a few hours later. When I heard the door buzz, I played as if I was very tired and slumped over with my hair over my face and my head hung low. I sat against the wall holding my knees loosely up to my chest.

As usual, he entered and started with his first and second questions. I didn't break my slumped stature as he asked where Asher was again and stood up seconds later heading for the door as he always did. Just before the buzz of the door, I sprang to my feet running as fast toward him as I could run. The rustle of my jumpsuit was the only sound that flashed and I was jumping through the air at him before he could turn around to see me.

The door buzzed and limped open several inches. I pulled my arm back and extended the palm of my hand as hard and as fast as I could as I lept through the air, pushing his face as it turned toward me and slamming his head against the edge of the heavy door. He fell to the ground instantly. I was shocked at myself for what I had done and that I was even able to do it.

A small pool of crimson started to expand around his wispy hairline, in stark contrast to the white everything. My whole life I had always been squeamish around blood, but I paused for a moment, reeling from what I had done and curiously mesmerized by the first color I had seen since I'd been here. I dragged the thin, bleeding doctor by the arm out of the way of the door's swing so I could get through. The warm blood left a streak like a paint brush stroke on the immaculate floors in a single stroke of desperate action.

I didn't have time to think at this point or dwell in remorse although I felt horrible about it. It was him or me I thought to myself. Dropping his hand after clearing his limp body from the door's path, I flung the door open and ran out the door to escape. I ran into the next room which was identical to the room I had been in, two rooms, one door, no exit. I fell to the floor screaming and crying uncontrollably.

"Nooooo"

I wailed as loud as I could, over and over. I didn't care who heard or what happened next. I cried until I was so physically tired that I fell asleep on the floor of the new room, not wanting to reenter my old room and having to face the reality of what I had done to the thin doctor.

When I woke after what seemed to be several hours later, longer than I usually sleep, I found myself in my same old room, the door sealed as it always was. My right tricep was sore and there was a small lesion the size of a pinhead where a new scab had formed. It hurt to touch; I felt a small bump under the skin there. I could tell it was my old room was because of the blood that was left in the room. The thin doctor was gone and I was left to my madness. The blood was mostly dried by now, but my guilt was still dripping.

I wanted my clean white room back at this point. I tore off my jumpsuit and fervidly tried to scrub what I had done off the floor and the edge of the door, which only made things worse. Most of the edges of the blood were already dried and the still wet parts in the center of where the thin doctor's head rested originally and where I had moved him to only smeared into a wider, area than had been there before. It became a bigger reminder of what I had done to him as well as my failed attempt at escaping this hell.

The temperature of the room was just cold enough to be uncomfortable and it didn't take long for me to remember this after removing my jumpsuit. It was the only clothing I had and there was no way I was putting that bloody thing back on. I was damned either way. I was naked and getting colder by the minute. I sat in my favorite corner and rocked myself to sleep to the sound of idle sobbing.

A few hours later, the food came through the slot as it always did, closing up automatically. I ignored the meal in spite of a nasty hunger, too upset to eat; I tried to go back to sleep. After a few more hours I was awoken again, this time by the steril buzz of the door.

I felt my body turn as white as the room as I wondered what was going to happen to me because of what I had done and who would be replacing the thin doctor. To my surprise, there was no replacement. Once again, the thin doctor entered the room as usual, straightening the thin wire frames of his glasses as he asked

"How are you feeling today?"

The question suddenly had new meaning and I almost answered. I wanted to apologize, but I didn't dare speak a word to this or his weather question. I just looked away in shame and fear. He squatted down on the balls of his feet less than a foot away from where I sat, closer than usual this time. He didn't say anything for nearly a minute; he just stared at me unwaveringly with a disgusted smile on his face.

I could only see this through the corner of my eye out from behind the thin veil of hair that was my only protection from him at this point. I had never felt more vulnerable; I didn't know what to expect. Just then, I heard the third question

"Where is Asher Wry?"

a voice spoke gruffly, but it was not the thin doctor's. My heart sunk into my stomach. I knew that voice and it was especially terrifying hearing it in this place. I heard steady footsteps approaching me now.

The question came again, this time louder and with more urgency

"Where is Asher, Candace?"

I looked up to see my father brooding over us both. The thin doctor changed his ugly smile to a genuine smile of delight as he rose from his perched stance and took a step back to the side and slightly behind my father.

"I won't ask a third time"

he said impatiently. He grabbed my arm just below my shoulder, yanking me to my feet. My father was an intimidating man at six foot four and 265 pounds.

"Come here"

he said as he continued to lead my body from his firm grip on me into the identical adjacent room. On the right of the room's wall, another door lurched open with the harsh buzz sound and we walked through into a long concrete hallway which was lit with a single continuous strip of green-tinged fluorescent lighting.

At the end of the cement hallway were a set of black metal double doors that led us into a laboratory were a dozen or more scientists were working at separate stations on what were very different kinds of projects, there was lab equipment, tools and computers and displays that plastered almost every open space on the surrounding walls.

We passed through the large lab through doors on the opposite ends of the room and entered into a long hallway that was filled with people in tiny office nooks working feverishly on computer terminals. There were definitely over a hundred of these little office cubicles that we passed before stepping into an elevator which took us for a short ride up.

The elevator dropped us off on a level with only a glass skywalk that led us through the dark industrial underbelly of a power plant or some huge engine room with endless pipes leading everywhere around the darkly lit skywalk. The other end led us out into a hallway with many different doors on either side down the vast corridor and we walked passed a few of the widely spaced doors before entering one door that was marked with a single letter "G" on the door.

He finally released his white knuckle grip from my arm for the first time since we started walking. My arm throbbed as the blood rushed back in and I felt my arm start to tingle like pins and needles when it falls to sleep. This room was more like a loungey boardroom. It had a large table in the center of the room and a living room type lounge off to the side.

"Sit."

he demanded as he released me in front of one of the end chairs, gesturing his finger down toward the chair. I quickly sat and he took a chair and faced it opposite of me and sat down.

"What were you doing with him?"

he asked.

"There are standards in this life. There is a reasonable expectation I have of people that share my same name, to protect its reputation. I don't think that includes fraternizing with the front page boy wonder who's solely known for protesting against me, to the point of riots on the grounds of my own buildings!"

The vein on the side of his neck always stuck out when he yelled. I always wondered if it was just going to pop one day while he was in the middle of screaming at somebody. All I could do was try to convince him I was listening and respecting what he had to say.

"I don't see you show the slightest bit of interest in a guy in four years and al the sudden, *he's* the one for you huh? I've got news for you; you're going to get exactly what you want, because you're going find him for me so we can have a little talk. It seems we lost touch when he didn't show up for our last meeting, I was expecting him."

"What do you want from him anyway? He may be pissed off with the way things are going in this world, but it's not like he's out to get *you*, he was just speaking his mind"

I said. He quickly rebutted

"words and beliefs are dangerous, more than you understand. People are sheep and they need to be treated like sheep. There's a reason they act like that, because they're stupid. They *need* someone to tell them what to do so they don't get separated from the flock, those that do, get eaten by wolves, wolves that are always ready to keep the boundary line tightly defined. Every flock can only have one Shepard. When people get distracted from the status quo and start listening to some kid rant about things he doesn't understand, it poses a problem, a problem that needs to be fixed."

"What, like you can just wish him away?" I said. He raised his eyebrow, looking intently at me.

"You can't just get rid of him, he's all people are talking about, especially since he *is* missing. People probably already suspect NanoCell of being behind this"

I said.

"Don't you think you'd know it if we did know where he was?"

he said snidely. It was the first thing that gave me hope since I'd last seen Asher, knowing that he was still free and safe somewhere.

"What would he talk to you about when you were together?"

he demanded.

"I don't know, normal things, movies, music, food"

I said.

"Cut the crap, did he talk about the government, NanoCell or any experiments he was doing?"

He said.

"He's into music theory and stuff, it's his major, why?"

I replied.

"He knows more than he should"

he said, cutting off the end of my sentence.

"Now listen"

he pointed his index finger in my face as he leaned closer to me.

"You're going to retrace your steps and find him for me; we need to come to an understanding on a few things. I'm going to give you 24 hours to make that happen. You'll be under watch by a security detail the whole time to ensure you keep up your end of the bargain."

he said.

"Bargain? What kind of a bargain is that?"

I said.

"The bargain is that I cancel the order for a room in a more permanent wing of the resort you've been staying at."

he replied.

"Why would you threaten me like this?"

I said, to which he replied

"Why would you betray your family?"

He was serious and he seriously believed that I could follow his reasoning. This was non-negotiable as far as he was concerned and it was my only ticket outside for a chance to hopefully find him and at least warn him.

"Go fix yourself"

he said, pointing off to the corner of the room where a rest room door was. I stood up and focused on remembering my posture lessons I had taken as a child and how much I hated them and rose to a regal posture nodded at him and walked into the bathroom. It had a shower and a change of clothes sitting on a shelf next to a clean folded towel. I took a dramatically necessary shower, dragging it on as long as I dared and got dressed.

There was a small bulge in the back pocket of my jeans and it made me crack a smile for a moment to find that it was a tube of red lipstick, but

"Why was it there?"

I thought. I didn't care; I was happy to have even a single luxury at this point. I walked out of the bathroom to hear the tail end of a phone call my father was having. He was speaking Hebrew in a very stern tone.

"Let's go"

he said as he gestured me to follow him. We walked through another long maze of doorways, halls and rooms before taking an elevator up to the lobby level of a downtown office building.

We walked out to the front of the building where a long motorcade of various black vehicles awaited. First a suburban, followed by my father's Maibach, then another suburban. My father and several of his security detail had met us at the door. He didn't even turn as he affirmatively barked "five o'clock, twenty four hours" as he stepped into the back of his waiting car. I was directed into a six series BMW.

My father and his entourage took off and I followed them onto the street with two more black cars following me. My father's car and one in front and behind his car veered off left while I kept straight to head uptown.

The drive gave me time to think, time to clear my head. The day light resurrected me and I felt new intense energy I had never felt before; I felt like I was being reborn. I stomped on the gas revving the engine and listening to it roar against the road for as long as traffic would allow.

The two cars following me didn't miss a beat, keeping pace each time I would do this. I just kept driving, reveling in my sudden freedom. I felt more and more torn as I got closer to Asher's apartment. I couldn't just throw him under the bus like my father wanted, but I couldn't go back to that sterile prison again either. I didn't doubt my father's words and was terrified to call his bluff.

I missed Asher more than my freedom at this point and just wanted to find him to be together again. He brought a side of me out that I had forgotten I *had* anymore and gave me hope, hope for a truer way of loving and being.

I finally arrived in front of Asher's building and drove around looking for a place to park. The two black SUV's were parked idling by my car as I walked up the steps to his building's entrance. I came to Asher's door and took a deep breath and rang the bell. An older Hispanic woman opened the door and asked

"Can I help you?"

"Hi, I'm looking for Asher, am I at the right place?"

I muttered. I looked around awkwardly at the door number and surroundings to be sure I was in the right place.

"You have the wrong place dear, I live alone."

She said.

"How long have you lived here?"

I asked as she began to close the door

"a few months now"

she responded just before the door shut completely.

"Oh, ma'am, can I ask you a couple more questions please?"

I said to the closed door, only to hear a trailing off

"bye bye"

from the other side of the door. My stomach sank as I turned to walk away.

"a few months?"

I mumbled to myself; it was an immediate reminder that I needed to find out what the date was to help get my bearings. I started back to my car to find out.

On the way out I passed the maintenance man

"Excuse me, I'm looking for Asher Wry, in 305, he used to live here?"

he looked puzzled for a minute, pulling and twisting the hairs of his dirty looking, black handle bar mustache.

"Hmm, 305. Yeah, I cleaned that one out a few months back, just up and left all his stuff, left it pretty trashed too I remember, punk. No one's claimed anything from that one either, got his boxes sitting in storage. If you find him, let him know I won't keep it forever and he's gonna need to settle up with the super before he can get it back"

"OK, thanks, I'll let him know if I find him, thanks"

I said as I was walking away. He was giving me the creeps, looking at me like I was dinner. He just stood there and watched me walk all the way down the hall and out the door. I walked quickly back to my car, looking over my shoulder for anything suspicious around me, but nothing was there.

I got in the car and started it, waiting for the car's dash interface to come up. I had worked myself up with anxiety over not being able to find Asher and frustrated with the two dead end conversations I'd just had.

The date on the dash indicated Thursday, October 19th. The 4th of July parade was one of the last big events I had been to the week prior to my abduction.

"Three months?"

I whispered to myself in disbelief. I starred at the screen in the dash as if to further process the implications. I was at a loss of where to look next for Asher, so I just started driving around to the places we'd been in a desperate attempt to find him with what little time I had.

I really didn't know much about his personal life. I only knew what we had together. It wasn't a long history, which made the strong emotional bond I had with him seem slightly out of place, but I couldn't help the way I felt about him. I had felt a magical kind of attraction to him even before we bonded that night with the starskin. I remembered the feeling I felt around him after that night, it was incredible. There was a definite difference. I remember that feeling was gone when I woke up in the white room; I just couldn't feel him around me anymore. It was like I was given wings for a day and then having them suddenly ripped off.

I drove around for hours searching all the streets and places we had been before returning to Asher's building and resorting to asking strangers on the street if they had seen or even knew him. No one was any help at all.

I didn't have my phone or anywhere else to look so I did a search for "Wry" through the car's dash interface and got a couple dozen results across the state.

I remembered Asher telling me he had family in Brooklyn, but didn't say who. There were only two results for that name in Brooklyn. I touched the first one to route the GPS based on my 50/50 odds. I raced to I-278 on my way to find "Michael Wry," in hopes he knew Asher.

Almost an hour later, I found myself wandering through Michael Wry's building. The door said "24 B" just like the listing said. I knocked quietly since it was just after midnight by now. I waited for a minute or two and knocked again on the sleeping door, a little louder now. I waited another minute and rang the bell. Just as I rang it the door flung open.

A thin and scruffy middle aged man was exaggerating how cold he was as he held his old wool blanket around his neck like a cape. He was only wearing boxers besides the blanket and I was clearly more embarrassed than he was.

"Who are you?"

he rightfully demanded, looking very disgruntled that he'd been woken up.

"Do you know what time it is?"

he grumbled.

"I'm really sorry to bother you, it's just, I'm looking for someone named Asher Wry and I was hoping you might know where I can find him."

I said meekly. There was a sincere trembling in my voice now that I was trying to hide.

"Asher doesn't live here, I'm his uncle. He hasn't lived around here for a couple years now, I don't see much of him anymore"

Michael said. I hung my head a little lower after hearing this.

"I'm sorry, wish I could help you, that's all I got"

he said.

"Well, thanks for your time, I'm really sorry for waking you up"

I said and turned away

"good luck"

he said and closed the door. I walked back to my car defeated again. I had lucked out on the first address I found and decided to try the second "Wry" listing I had, since I was in the area "Harry and Joanne Wry." I pushed the second listing to route my GPS again and found the address only a few minutes away.

There was a flashing TV light going on in the front room as I approached the door so I didn't feel as bad knocking as it looked like someone was awake here. I knocked and quickly got an answer, they didn't know anyone named Asher. With nothing else to go on, I drove back toward Harlem.

I stopped at a gas station and asked to borrow a pen and paper. I pulled up in front of Asher's building again and placed the scrawled-on paper that read

"Asher Wry?"

under one of the wiper blades. I got back in the car and curled up in the passenger's front seat and went to sleep with the dim glow from the yellow fog lights in my eyes from the cars that had been following me all day.

I was awoken by a man knocking on my window. I looked around startlingly and saw him motioning to roll down my window. I rolled the window down just a crack to safely talk to him since I didn't recognize him.

"Do you know Asher"

he said

"Yes, do you?"

I replied.

"Yeah, he's my friend. I haven't seen him for a while, I've been really worried about him, it's like he just disappeared. I'm Lars by the way, and you are?"

He sustained his last word, waiting for my answer.

"I'm Candace, we're friends and I really just need to talk to him as soon as possible. So, you don't have any idea where he would be?"

I asked.

"No clue. He's usually a home body and only goes out when he has too. Last time I talked to him he was on his way over to my place to help me move, but he never showed up"

he said. We talked a bit more and put together a loose timeline and I explained that I had been with him after that and that I'd been "away" for a while and concluding that neither of us had seen him at all recently. We quickly picked up on each other's concern for Asher.

"Do you want to grab some coffee and talk, my treat?"

he asked. I was cold from the night and starving.

"Okay"

I said. We walked a couple of blocks away from where I was parked and found a tiny diner and sat down to talk.

Lars was looking over the menu

"You hungry?"

He asked

"Starving, just a little short on credits at the moment"

I replied.

"Don't worry about it, get what you want" I felt like a bum. It was one of the only times in my life that I felt truly humbled; I gave Lars a kind smile to thank him, he reciprocated and looked back to his menu

"hmm, what sounds good?"

he asked.

"I'm fine with whatever"

I replied. Our waitress came by again and took our order. Lars just ordered a varied spread of a la carte breakfast foods that we both pecked at as we talked.

We talked about Asher and shared stories we had each never heard about our missing friend. I told him about our brief yet rich time we spent with each other and Lars gave me a much better impression of what he was like when he was younger, his interests and a few embarrassing and exciting adventures they'd been though together as teenagers.

I told him about how he was detained for a couple of weeks after the riots first started and that he was released for a while then detained again.

"I know, it's been all over the news and all anyone's talking about online. The police haven't made any announcements and the news hasn't given any real information about when he's going to be released, just that he was jailed again for inciting a riot"

"Can you believe that crap?"

A man sitting at the diner bar turned around to comment on our conversation. This caught us both off guard a little, but wasn't an offensive intrusion since he was very adamant about agreeing with us. Lars and I both stopped to acknowledge him. "He's a stand-up guy, trust me"

the man said confidently.

"Do you know him?"

Lars asked

"Oh yeah, I mean I kind of met him when we were both protesting before the riots started. He followed me up on the horn about what I was saying about my dad. He really got people fired-up about everything that's wrong right now."

"So you don't actually *know* him right?" Lars said

"Hey man, I *respect* him and that's all I need to know. A lot more than I can say for most people"

The man got a little defensive, but quickly embarrassed himself for getting worked up.

"Hey, I agree, just asking"

Lars said with a smile.

"I'm sorry, I just take it seriously when I see the rich getting richer and the poorer getting poorer and our freedoms are being stripped away one by one. Pretty soon we won't have any rights left to defend and to make things worse, no one is ever held accountable, there's no balance."

He extended his hand to Lars and said "Danny Roberts, mind if I sit down?"

"No, not at all, Lars Fohlm, good to meet you"

he said motioning with one hand to sit while shaking his hand, he followed suit with me shaking my hand

"Candace, pleased to meet you."

He pulled up a chair and sat in it reversely. I was nervous and hoped there wasn't the follow up question for my last name. I felt like a sheep amongst wolves at times because of my name, it wasn't always a pleasant thing to be a Vanderbilt. The question wasn't asked and they jumped right into discussing their views of how the system we lived in was broken.

"There's all this talk about what's wrong and everyone's pointing fingers, but when it comes right down to it, nothing is happening because everyone is so dead set in their ultra-convenient consumer ways"

Danny said

"Everyone likes to complain about how bad things are, but no one wants to get off their ass and do the work to make a change for something different, something better. Everyone wants the same thing, everyone wants to live comfortably and not want for anything and to just be happy, but that's the problem. It seems basic, it seems possible, but the distribution is just all screwed up now. The curve keeps getting steeper and steeper, 99.9% of the world's wealth is held by less than one percent of the world's population. The golden rule is those who have the gold, make the rules, how is that right on any level?"

Danny was intensely animated, it was obvious he was extremely passionate about what he was talking about. Lars responded

"Right, but what do you purpose? It could be argued that those that have the gold earned it by years of hard work in a free market and sure, luck and the occasional corporate backstabbing, but earned on the labor of a man's own hard work and dedication."

Danny sat with a stunned look on his face, mouth agape and rebuffed

"Are you being serious right now? Anyone who could stand there and tell me that he believed that crap is no man I want to be talking to or live in the same community with. Frankly, that person is the problem. The complacent sheep who believes what they're fed by the media, no questions asked. It's the same person that would willingly trade freedom for security and that, my friend, is a grave mistake."

"I agree"

I felt I truly understood where he was coming from.

"Me too"

Lars said. He was intently listening to Danny; his body language suggested he was eager to hear more, as was I. Danny's face turned serious and introverted, almost cathartic.

"There needs to be a voice, a single light that people can follow. It's pitch black out there and no one knows where they're going. We're better than this, as a species. We owe it to our children. It makes me sick to think of my little girl growing up in a world that will be worse than the darkness I've seen. Unless we wake up and come together to change what's wrong now, there won't be any turning back."

The air was suddenly thick and silent even though the busy diner buzzed and clanged on behind us. We just looked at each other and down as if ashamed, recalling our own lack of efforts.

"No matter what we do, it doesn't matter unless a change is affected"

I spoke slowly in a dazed monotone as I kept my eyes in a locked and unfocused position on a gouge in the table top.

"You are exactly right"

I continued. I snapped out of my stare, perked up in my chair.

"We need to find Asher, now"

I said in a sudden urgency and locked eyes with a razor focus on Danny and then Lars. I felt I had let too much time slip away already.

"I can help."

Danny nodded confidently.

"I'm sorry I can't help today, I'm running late for work, but please keep me in the loop, I want to help, I just can't right now."

He handed each of us a business card and shook our hands.

"It was very good to meet you both"

He smiled again as he left and I reciprocated.

"See, that's what I mean, everybody's always too busy and it's not his fault, we're kept in the wheel chasing virtual cheese by design and... I'm sorry, I'm rambling, I tend to do that so just tell me to shut up."

He looked like he was scolding himself.

"No, it's fine; I really like hearing your point of view, it's actually quite refreshing to hear that side of things."

I said.

"As opposed to always hearing about how the one percent have it rough?"

he laughed out loud. My face couldn't hide the awkwardness I felt.

"Candace?"

he said quizzically. I paused. "My father is Conrad Vanderbilt"

Danny's countenance flipped to disgust

"What is this some kind of setup?"

he said aggressively as he sat up straight in his chair holding his hands up in front of him.

"No, no, I'm sorry, I know I'm not winning a popularity contest with a lot of people, but trust me that's not who *I* am, I don't think like him and I don't act like him, he disgusts me."

"Trust you, you say? Isn't that pretty much the one percent's club motto? Trust me, everything will be just fine, just like it is now, but even better"

he sneered. I took a moment and looked down as I gathered my thoughts; trying to choose my next words carefully.

"Look, I'm sorry that I was born into that kind of family. I've been appalled after finding out the kinds of people they are and the company they keep just like anyone with a soul would, but I can't help..."

He interrupted me mid-sentence.

"You continuing to participate in that lifestyle and associate yourself with it despite being disgusted by it is proof that you're not that disgusted by it"

"I'm sorry, I shouldn't have..."

he said as I interjected

"No, you're absolutely right and it goes along with what you were saying about people just being too lazy and complacent. It's too easy for most people to resist the path of least resistance. Look, I'm not them ok? See that black suburban right there? I pointed out the front window kiddy corner to the diner.

"Had my eye on it all morning. The best defense is a good offense. It's not the first time

I've been watched. You can't be in *everyone's* good graces right?"

He said.

"Actually that one's for me and I only have a few hours left before they pick me up and take me back there."

A short gasp and few tears escaped my grasp

"Who, take you back where?"

I leaned in closer to Danny, trying to compose myself, wiping the tears from the sides of my eyes.

"My father has been holding and interrogating me in a cell in one of his secret underground facilities for months now up until yesterday when he gave me exactly 24 hours to bring him Asher." Danny was listening.

"I don't know how or where to look now, I'm running out of time and options; I've looked everywhere I can think of already, retraced all my steps, even talked to his family, no one has seen him for months either, I don't even know if he's alive."

I just broke down and cried, not trying to fight it anymore.

"Hey, come on, it's ok"

Danny said as he extended his hand and gently touched my shoulder. His hands were warm; it was so nice to have a human connection again, just being around a good person was a born-again experience. I cried with my hands in my face for a few minutes, making a scene of myself, but I didn't care and neither did Danny. I tried to breathe and smile to try to compose myself as I wiped away the stream of tears that soaked my napkin. I took several deep, slow breaths. Danny was just patiently smiling.

"Wow, I'm sorry, I just…"

"You don't have to explain"

he interrupted. I smiled and sighed in relief that he said that

"Thanks. So, I guess that's all I've got going on, what are your plans for the day Mr. Roberts?"

He smiled and said

"Helping a friend"

He stood up and extended his hand to help me up.

Ch. 6
| mercy |

I was pleasantly surprised by his good manners.

"Where to first?"

He asked.

"Anywhere. Any Ideas?"

I said. We walked out of the diner and onto the sidewalk.

"I'll drive, I'm parked over here"

I was reluctant since I had just met him, but needed all the help I could get at this point.

"No, it's ok, I'll drive; my car's close."

"Oh come on, I'm the least of your worries, relax"

he joked. I smiled back at him

"I'll drive *your* car"

I said.

"Deal, if you're up to it"

he said as he threw his keys up in the air which I confidently gleaned right out of the sky and glared a smile at him.

"Right here"

he said pointing to a very intimidating looking pickup truck. I immediately regretted volunteering myself.

"Seriously? Did you get this from a monster truck rally?"

I was expecting an actual car, not a supped-up truck with king-sized tires. The biggest thing I had ever driven was a catering minivan that I had to help back up a few feet once. I swallowed hard, hit the remote locks and literally climbed into the driver's seat using the handles and side steps that were custom installed for this purpose.

Danny offered to help but I was already up by the time he got near. We both got in and buckled up.

"So, what possessed you to buy this beast? It's only slightly out of place in the city."

I said.

"I don't know, I just always wanted one and being able to see over traffic is a definite bonus."

His humor put me at ease a bit as I set off down the street in awkward fashion. The huge truck lumbered forward, the massive tires made a loud humming in the otherwise quiet cab. Looking in the rearview mirror, I saw that it did not take long for the black suburban to begin tailing Danny's truck. I wasn't surprised, but felt like this was a good time to tell him

"Just so you know, I don't think our tail is one we're going to be able to shake."

Danny raised an eyebrow at me

"Want me to drive?"

he said.

"No, it's not that, I have a... an implant, under my skin."

I centered my left hand on the wheel and lifted my right arm up to show Danny the scab on the back of my arm.

"See."

He grimaced a bit and breathed in making a "Ssssss" sound.

"Shouldn't be too bad."

He said as he inspected it closer. He reached out with his forefinger

"Oww, it's just really sore."

I reminded him

"Sorry, I'm just looking. It's really red; it doesn't want to be in there does it?"

He said rhetorically.

"No, it doesn't, the feeling's mutual, trust me."

I was trying to control my stress levels, but my sarcasm was getting the best of me.

"We can fix that, my sister's a doctor at a hospital near the park. Head over to Madison and keep heading uptown; I'm texting her now"

He looked at me with a gentle smile

"You're pretty cool hand Luke huh?"

I said.

"Nah, it's easy to be collected looking at a problem from the outside in. I just like to help where I can."

He was quiet for most of the rest of the drive except for giving me directions to the hospital. He looked noticeably concerned and had a soft spoken confidence.

"It's on the right up here, just park right in the front."

he said. Our unwanted followers had not strayed from their assignment, parking across the street, ever vigilant. We walked up the handicap ramp to the hospital entrance, past the front desk into the labyrinth of halls. We ended up at an office at the end of the fifth or so hall we trudged down. It was all glass including a massive door, which Danny opened for me.

"Hi, we're here to see Dr. Seibel."

He said.

"Danny right? She's been expecting you. Right this way"

"I messaged her on the way"

He whispered. The receptionist motioned to a waiting nurse who led us into a patient room where we waited for his sister no more than five minutes

"Danny, oh it's so good to see you"

she said enthusiastically as she hugged him.

"And you must be Candace, jeez, I see what you mean, she's gorgeous"

she said winking at him

"Shut up Audrey"

he said, he was clearly embarrassed, which made he and I both blush and feel slightly awkward at the same time.

"Um, anyway, go ahead, show her"

he said. I turned my back and produced the back of my arm to her; I cringed at her light probing while inspecting it

"What happened?"

she said with a puzzled face. I told her the same story I had told Danny.

"Huh, well that's a new one. I guess we'll just have to take a look. This should be easy and quick. I'll give you a couple of small shots to numb the area and I'll be able to remove whatever's in there, ok."

She smiled and got to work and in less than a minute there was a clank on the metal tray next the examination table, an eerie, haunting feeling came over all of us.

My eyes became watery. Audrey had a look of terror looking down at the micro light pulse emitting from the tiny device. I was feeling a cold sweat in full swing at this point

"Flush it. It's the only way to get it away from us, as far away as possible"

Danny said. I was looking down, breathing hard, taking in the gravity of the situation.

"We need to get out of here. We can't stay, they'll figure it out."

Danny said as he sprang to his feet.

"trade me cars, I'm out front."

He put his keys in Audrey's hands and she went for hers in her purse. She returned in seconds with her keys.

"Be safe, don't be stupid Danny. It was nice to meet you, maybe we'll have dinner next time instead?"

she said smiling.

"Thank you, so much."

I said. We heard a

"good luck"

as we left down the hall and out the office into the hallway.

"This way"

Danny pointed the opposite way than we had come and led us down into the parking garage where we roamed around for several minutes looking until we found her silver Volvo. We exited on the back side of the hospital which happened to be on the other side of the block than we had originally parked, implant free.

We headed out of the way a few blocks to avoid our tail as much as possible and it worked; we were free and clear as we headed back down to Brooklyn where Danny lived. We were sweating bullets the whole drive back and couldn't believe it when the garage door was finally closed behind us. We sat there for a few seconds in the darkened garage lit with the single light from the garage door opener until it automatically turned off.

Danny opened the door and the car light turned on and he laughed

"come on."

We went into the house and he opened the fridge and offered me a seat in the living room that was adjacent to the open kitchen. I sat in a big comfy arm chair.

"Want are you drinking?"

he said as he cracked open a beer.

"Do you have any water or juice?"

I replied.

"OJ it is."

he said as he sat down next to me, handing me the juice. It was delicious. I almost drank it all in a single breath, but reached to set the rest down on the coffee table in front of us.

"Uh uh uh..."

Danny motioned me back and put all five finger tips of his right hand on the top left corner of the surface, turning them counter clockwise a quarter of a turn and the whole table lit up like slot machine. The giant touch screen table was filled with real-time streaming data of every kind, monitoring everything from weather to stock markets to terror warnings to closed circuit cameras and satellite imaging.

"It looks like I came to the right place."

I said, he just smiled in return

"Yes you did, now when and where did you last see Mr. Wry"

he said.

"I guess about three months ago, in Columbus Circle Station on 59th."

"OK, that shouldn't be too hard, that place is crawling with cameras. We just need to narrow down the day and time now."

He handed me a smaller handheld tablet to use. I looked through the calendar tracing back the last things that I could pin down a date for before I was taken that day in the subway station. While I was digging through dates, Danny was busy typing into some kind of command line.

"What are you doing"

I said, pausing and looking over the tablet. It was amazing watching how fast he typed and what the screen of text and scripts that were running, almost as if it was playing out some kind of epileptic dance on the display.

"Just accessing a handy little database that a buddy and I put together. It's access to all of the city's closed circuit camera streams and archives and over half of the private cameras; there's more than 30,000 cameras here."

It didn't take long before he had pulled up the 59th street cameras and was waiting on me for a date and time.

"June 29th, 9:00 AM, start there I guess"

I said. A newfound seriousness came over me. Danny was exactly the weapon I needed.

144

"So, this *friend* isn't exactly law enforcement, is he?"

He looked at me devilishly and continued to talk and type

"I guess that depends on what you mean by law enforcement. He's definitely not a cop."

He said laughing as if trying to control it.

"But he does enforce laws, or rather rights. He speeds up the natural progression of natural laws, we all do."

"Who is we, what do you mean?"

I said with genuine sincerity, not wanting to feel stupid at this point. For some reason his cryptic response didn't register.

"The majority's. The majority of people in this world that have been disenfranchised by the minority in power who would rather see the earth and all its inhabitants die at their feet before sharing its resources or power. For thousands of years, humans have been enslaved by ruling masters under the guise of freedom. Now things are different, now we finally have leverage to even the playing field. We exploit the fact that even the masters of this world are now completely reliant on the crutch of technology. Just like Robin Hood, we use our skill and our speed to take back freedoms that get exploited or taken from us as a majority and to remind the royal hand that they cannot take honey from the hive without being stung. The SafetyNet ACT made it

145

completely up to the discretion of government officials as to what kind of data they are allowed to monitor and abuse in the name of national security so we have no choice but to arm and defend ourselves. We think of it as a technological clause addendum to the 2nd amendment."

I was stunned.

"Anonymous, of course."

I said.

"Well yeah, we don't really love the label, but that's what the media calls us and it serves its purpose"

he said hesitantly; we both laughed.

"Speaking of, looks like 0dys3us has found what he was looking for."

The results on his terminal session had come to a stop and he loaded up a site that we could view the results on from that morning. We scanned through the video at varying speeds to save time, looking at an angle of video from a surveillance camera where we could see the bench that we were sitting on. We went over the footage three times over the next hour or so for time period that we would have been there.

"This is so frustrating."

I said

"Hey, if you think you can find it faster, please, be my guest. This is like finding a needle in a haystack and I only know which haystack to look in based off what you're telling me."

He said with a raised eyebrow.

"No, I'm sorry, I just mean this whole thing in general, I don't mean that at you."

"Maybe you just have the day wrong" he said.

"No, I don't think so, I'm sure it was the 29th."

"Let me just check a few things" he said. He went to work back in his command line terminal and started typing feverishly away at it. He was looking for something specific, digging through dense layers of subdirectories. He kept at this for a few minutes before opening up a second identical window.

"Here, look. The file for the 29th, it's the same size as the 28th."

He was showing me the two files.

"So, they are the same 24 hour period, they *should* be the same size" I said.

"Yeah, but not exactly the same size, down to the byte. Even in a recording time period that is exactly the same time, the files are still slightly different when you look at byte size. Look at this, the time stamp is a different time of day than the recording system would have automatically archived the day's recordings at. See, the system automatically archives the previous day's files at 12:01 AM every day and the file for the 29th has a time stamp of 11:56 AM that same day, about two hours after you would have been there."

He went checking around again for a few minutes on the other terminal screen he had pulled up on the other side of the display.

"There is no log entry for that archival taking place at 12:01 on the 30th. That video was intentionally removed and replaced with a copy of the 28th's video archive."

He said all this very casually, I was shocked at what he was able to find.

"Not too surprising and sloppy to be honest, but someone is definitely hiding something because the only people that have access to these cameras are high level people at MTA and the police, so whoever did this is hiding it from even them. Tracking them down is probably possible, but it would take some time and even then can lead to dead ends because of VPN's, proxies and public access computers, it depends."

"No, there's no time for that, I'm sure we've both got a pretty good idea about who it was, but now we're back to square one and no closer to finding Asher"

I was defeated and honestly out of ideas and hope.

"Well at least we have a little more time now with your implant out. What will you do when you find him?"

he asked. I paused for a moment, not really sure of how to answer now.

"Hug him; see if he hugs me back…"

"And if he doesn't?"

Danny asked.

"If he *does*…"

I fired back.

"If he does, I'm hoping maybe he'll want to leave town with me."

I realized how ridiculous that sounded after saying it. I was kidding myself and expecting to be mocked.

"Hope is what makes us human, I'm glad you still have some left."

It was profound and touching and most of all unexpected.

"Thank you"

I said, smiling timidly. There was a short pause, but it was warm, not awkward at all.

"Well, this shouldn't stop us from eating right? We'll need our strength to keep up the good fight."

Danny walked over to the freezer and pulled out some frozen pocket meals

"Pepperoni or Philly Cheese Steak?"

He asked. I felt my stomach turn just by looking at them.

"I know, but I'm a bachelor and a hobbit, not exactly a recipe for gourmet, what do you do?"

I walked over to him to examine both packages trying to discern the lesser of two evils.

"When in Rome…"

I poked at the Pepperoni box with joking contempt as we both laughed. Danny prepped our low-brow meals while I wandered out the back door onto the wooden deck. The yard was surrounded by tall old trees that pretty well enclosed the whole backyard.

I was surrounded by the sound of the light wind moving through the leaves and soon was feeling hot from the midday sun almost directly overhead now. I looked up toward the sky with my eyes closed, the bright light of the sun illuminating my eyes and mind. The familiar smells of summer filled me with a calming peace as inhaled and exhaled slowly, it was a memorable moment since it had been so long since it had this common sensation I had always taken for granted.

"Lunch is served madam"

Danny's footsteps on the deck snapped me out of my summer daze. He was walking toward me with a large tray that had our food and two jangling ice waters. He set the tray down on the little table between the padded lawn chairs.

"Sorry about the setup, I don't have company over often, especially pretty ladies like you."

I blushed.

"Thank you."

I said with a smile before hiding behind my clear glass of water. I could tell he had built up courage to say something like that. I thought it was sweet, but I hoped he wasn't getting the wrong idea as I just wasn't in that frame of mind, at all. He wasn't being inappropriate or creepy, he just seemed lonely. We talked about the weather and just admired the day as we started eating.

"So what do you like to do... I mean when you're not playing Candace P.I.?"

"Well, I don't know, I don't usually have a lot of downtime. I spend most of my time in class or studying, but I try to fit in sleep, lemon gelato and T'ai chi where I can. What about you?"

I replied.

"I do a lot of sys admin and I.T. work, I freelance mostly, but the pay is somehow steady so it works. I like photography. I like being in nature and seeing life from unexpected angles. I try to show common things in an uncommon setting or from a unique point of view, after all, that's all that really matters to people is their own point of view. I just try to satisfy that innate need in everyone, to help them recognize the beauty that they might not otherwise notice."

"I think that's very noble. It's the little things that make or break us and give meaning to us."

I replied. I was very relaxed at this point and quite happy with the way the conversation was going. Danny had a look of concern.

"What's wrong?"

I asked. He raised his index finger as if to pause the conversation.

"W-What?"

Danny shushed me, still with his finger out, his eyes fixed sharply to the side and his head cocked the opposite direction.

"That low hum, do you hear it?"

I paused again intently listening for the sound he was talking about.

"I waited for a moment silently."

"Yeah, I do now"

The hum was getting deeper and louder and the sound grew more defined and choppy. The hum kept getting louder and soon turned into flapping. Danny broke his concentration and looked over at me again

"I have a very bad feeling about this. We should go, now."

Danny said as he motioned me up. The sounds were growing so loud now we could hear them from inside the house as we walked in to make our way out to the garage. We jumped back in the car as fast as we could. Light from the opening garage door started to pour into the black garage and everything except the radio antenna on his car cleared the bottom of the rising garage door, barely. I focused on the wiggling antenna as Danny ripped out of his driveway onto the street.

He floored it for only a second before lifting off the accelerator. By this time there were three military helicopters hovering above us and a barrage of military and police vehicles careening toward us from both ends of the street. He threw the car into park yelling enough colorful curse words for each vehicle to adopt a few as their own. A very loud speaker came on over all the noise.

"This is the United States Army, you are surrounded, exit the vehicle and lay face down on the ground now, I repeat, exit the vehicle and lay face down on the ground now. You have 10 seconds to comply before being fired upon. Ten, Nine…"

The voice over the helicopter's intercom did not get to seven before we were both on the ground face down with combat boots running toward us. I looked over toward Danny under the car. He had begun to tear up, repeating

"I'm sorry"

over and over and I couldn't help but feel the same.

Ch. 7
| the void |

I started to sit down after a few minutes of not knowing what to say or do, but I was a bit tired from the stress and walking.

"No, do not sit Asher"

Vasha synced to me.

"They are coming"

I stood there waiting and watching the sphere's waves dance around, they were calming to watch, hypnotic even. To my left, there was a small pin light that appeared which immediately caught my attention not because of its size, but because of how bright it was; like the shine of a mirror reflecting the sun in your eyes.

The immense pin light was immediately followed by the hum of a low, pure tone. It was the most pristine sound I'd ever heard. Unwavering, the sound turned the pin light red which had now spread into a pipe of ruby red light, extending as high and low as I could see.

As soon as the light had fully expanded, another pin light appeared a few paces away, followed by another loud, pure tone. The pitch was slightly higher coming from this light, but just as loud and just as clean. They resonated in perfect harmony together. The pin light that birthed this sound shot into an orange pipe of light, just like the first. The process continued all around us, next with a yellow pipe of light and making an even higher pitch, then green, blue and purple, all with ever increasing pitches.

Even with six distinctly different pitches sounding at once, none of them strayed from a perfect harmonious tone that erupted into a tone that blocked out all sound and even thought. I could only observe disconnected. A much larger pipe of white light appeared and passed directly through us where we stood in the middle of the great sphere.

I was immediately absorbed in the beam of light. I wasn't gone, I wasn't anywhere; I was, everywhere, floating as everything in everything. I reached out close to me and I was able, I reached out for miles and it was there. I felt no limitations; every movement was a matter of will alone. I could not see myself in a physical form, yet I could reach out and touch anything and would feel every part of everything, everywhere.

My consciousness, will and being were all one with everything. I felt completely loose and floating like being underwater, but with precision focus and control. This was much different than the strong feelings and connection from syncing because it was also the ability to manipulate anything as I wanted. Whatever I thought became my reality. My environment was a blank canvas for my mind to paint and manipulate. It was a god-like reality.

I thought of sitting on a rock in low earth orbit and I was; I reached down toward the earth and the closer I willed it, the closer I became. I reached down and plucked a single grape from a vineyard on earth and slightly corrected my posture, just as easily as if I were grabbing anything at arm's length.

I looked to my left on the ground and picked up a strangely fractaled ice crystal; to my right I scooped a handful of solar fire from the sun. I smashed them together and they shattered into millions of fine diamonds which began morphing into a liquid, dripping down in the form of blood from the base of my loosely touching palms. Down both of my forearms, blood dripped off my elbows, each droplet transfigured into a beautiful white and pink orchid mantis and gliding off into the vastness of space.

In every direction was endlessly attainable time and dimension, but it was all understated by the light and dark concentrations. They were like clouds, intricate, chaotic patterns of varying intensities. The basic and complex were all bound and governed by the single law of intent; it's what ultimately defines us. Intent is how one's frequency is tuned.

I cleared my mind. The scale of what I was viewing was too immense for words to do justice. I was seeing the totality of the universe and of all time from an empty distance. From the side, time seemed to move linearly, left to right, past to future respectively. When I moved around the focal point of the complete universe, I saw the perpetual wave of time that is always circulating, mixing and evolving within itself, swirling around like earth's equator and weaving through that constant wave of *time* was a constant *dimensional* wave that was moving around the universe vertically, up one side and revolving down the other.

Both perpendicular motions flowed harmoniously through each other creating a constantly unique nature. The dark intent clouding of human history was not even visible from this vantage point. Zooming into modern human history revealed great concentrations of light and dark patches specifically grouped around historically prominent times in our global history.

The intent concentration patching looked blotchy from far back, there was no rhyme or reason to them, almost resembling early DNA profiles and stacked infinitely on top of each other in endless combinations of dimensions for them to coexist with.

There were a few spots where the light signature was so bright at certain points of time that it pierced through all the dimensional layers and not just the single dimension that most of the intent patches existed on. It looked like a white slice mark through the universe like a knife through an orange. These few instances were moments in time that god divinely intervened.

In the dimension that the vast majority of the activity was showing, the space and time stretched side to side, front to back. I was attracted to the great library of Alexandria's light, then to Buddha's founding and the crowning of medieval kings. I also saw the darkness. I felt the discordant frequencies that gave it its color.

I visited Babylon, Sodom and Gomorrah and WWII Germany. They were all low lights of positive intent. I found it troubling that before human history, it was pure light, during, there were dark patches, but toward the future, it wasn't dark, but there was a kind of forward bleed of dark intent protruding into the future past our present time. It was a dark premonition on a literal scale.

Intent is focused and controlled agency that we exercise and therefore can be changed; it must be changed if it is not in harmony.

I had seen enough for now and was instantly back in the sphere with Vasha. I looked around now at the six majestic Atlantians that surrounded us. They were all spaced evenly apart around the perimeter of the sphere. They were not like Nelis or our escorts. They deeply resembled them, but also like the beings of light we had seen earlier, they had light auras, but theirs were the same colors as the pipes of light that were just there a moment ago... a moment that I was able to return to.

There was no discussion or question from the Atlantians as I had anticipated before coming here. It was clear I had their attention and respect. All at once, the Atlantians auras silently flashed their respective colored lights which seemed to envelope the beings, disappearing into the pin light from which they came. Vasha looked at me with adoration and pride.

Positive energy flowed from her into me at a terrific rate creating an unbreakable sync that bonded us. I felt our hearts sync up as we closed our eyes. After a couple combined beats, we felt our heartbeat sync with the earth's heartbeat. We opened our eyes and found ourselves in the throne room and heart of the earth, the inner sun. Our hearts raced faster together. The earth's heart was following ours, not the other way around.

We swelled with energy and it followed suite beating syncopatically with us and lulling with our tide.

"Thank you, for everything."

I said. Vasha was beaming with energy.

"Thank you Asher, for your light."

We were saying goodbye, but I laughed and relished the irony that we are never apart as one.

"I'm here."

She said with her soft smile and I was gone.

Back on the surface, rounding the corner where I used to live, nothing had changed, but everything was different; everything was reborn and everything was possible. As I looked around at my familiar, yet alien surroundings, it became apparent very quickly that I preferred not to let my mind wonder too much.

I passed the hot dog cart that historically sold from the corner opposite my old building; the smell was familiar and savory. I thought of how many times I had eaten dinner there when I was stretched thin and I was instantly there. I was back in the past, experiencing the past reality as myself, but from an elevated consciousness that my past self was not aware of during this kind of temporary self-possession.

I was there, laughing with Lars, watching all the girls walk by, too shy to ever talk to them. The two of us would just stand there against the building talking about which ones we liked We talked about what annoyed us and what inspired us, easily eating two or three hot dogs each. The smell took me there.

The slight impulse that scent alone created in my brain was enough to cause my body to omnisciently evoke that to be my reality, in the exact time and dimension that that past reality existed. I was easily able to revert back into the present reality; it was more of an oddity or "note to self" moment than anything although the memory was nice. It was nostalgic and made me miss past simplicities.

All around me I could sense the past and people all around me, layer upon layer of possible moments played out in endless dimensions. It was all the "shoulda, woulda, coulda's". It was an omnipresent state of "what if?"

There was a woman in a red dress on the street corner having a conversation with a man in a tailored suit in one dimension where she is laughing, another dimension where she is screaming in terror, trying to run from the man and another dimension where the man is there with a different woman. There was every possibility of every situation happening all at once and within my perception.

This state was what was happening all around me when I was thinking passively. It was engagingly immersive. It was also not an issue blocking it out either; I could just will the perception there or not.

I kept walking down the streets I had been on countless times before, seeing everything with new eyes and feeling everything around me with a new found harmonic reverence. I was feeling the energies of everything around me, from all times and dimensions of every specific place I stepped. It was still as alive as each moment ever was, still happening, as it was or was to be happening.

All of that focused energy was flowing into me and I was backscattering it as a positive cymatic wave a thousand fold. Just feeling that surge of each event happening all around me as I passed through it was endlessly deep; a connected experience I could feel coursing through the universe and myself like lightning in my veins.

I felt all the pain and all the pleasure. The more I would switch between this perception and "reality" the more I was intrigued. I began drifting in thought and slipping forward in place on the street I was walking. I would think to be 50 yards or thirty miles further ahead and I seamlessly morphed to that place. There were a lot of double takes. I got a kick out of the confused reactions people gave me when they were sure I wasn't there a moment ago. I just smiled at them and moved on; silence is golden.

This slipping between places was an addicting sensation; it got me thinking of so many ways to have fun. Conrad hadn't been playing very nice and he was way over due for a reality check. I focused on Conrad in my mind and his entire life path emerged to me like a map overlay in my expanded dimensional vision. Reality and outside focus faded away and I was left with Conrad's timeline which showed not only the path he had travelled in life, but everything he had been and was currently connected to.

I saw a bland and straight forward lifeline he was traveling until his early twenties, where his connection branches exploded outward into a chaotic network of other nefarious characters he had aligned himself with. His line was a dense web of darkness that a lot of people, corporations and politicians were all connected to and were all down the line from him. He was not the end of his own line either though. He was also connected to other dark people and energies that he was down the line from.

This hierarchical pedigree view of the ways in which we are all connected was clear. There were 11 others that I recognized to be on a similar level to Conrad throughout the world and only three humans above them, beyond that, I felt the pure cacophonous frequency that is the darkness we fear as humans. The evil that infects men directly stemmed from a dark and unearthly Draconian resonance that had been manipulating the will of man from the beginning of human history.

The disharmonic nature of its cymatic signature was as boldly out of place as the devil in church. It was clear from this view what the poison was and where it flowed. Greed, corruption, power and everything else negative in the world was constantly being crafted manipulated to evolve with us.

Every time the human race would advance spiritually, the dark frequency was changed and kept in stark contrast to the positive spiritual energy that humans were trying to ascend to, it kept humans in a constant negative state. It was the morphing antithesis of all that was good. The crude level of spirituality that the dark frequency maintained us at, kept us from advancing and kept us stagnant and limited in this world and dimension.

It kept us from shining our inherently white light unless great steps were taken by an individual to try to block it out as much as possible in hopes of gaining the smallest amount of clarity and even then it was stifled. The Draconians, their three subservient hidden masters and the twelve world power players were at the root of everything that is wrong with the world, the reason that 99% of the world's population was in the rut that they had not ever been able to escape.

It was clear it was an intentional manipulative act in order to satisfy their insatiable lust for control and resources. Just as it was human nature in the past to trade freedom for security, those 15 humans in power were equally susceptible to the Draconians influence and the cycle continued through over a hundred generations. As I scanned over the political and commercial web that enveloped the planet, nearly every motive was the same and all led back to this darkness.

All the largest corporations that constantly bombarded people with engrained symbolism and subliminal dark frequencies all led back to these same 15 humans that had their hand in pulling their corporate and in turn, political strings.

The Draconians had been here since the beginning of man, from the moment they knew of our existence. They came to earth thousands of years ago. The Atlantians had also been here for nearly as long, although they came just after they had learned the Draconians had come here only to find that they had already exercised control over our human race and had enmeshed their dark frequency in the earth which the Atlantians could not reverse without harming the earth.

The Atlantians and Draconians shared similar technologies, some of which were stolen by the Draconians from the Atlantians long before humans were in the picture. The Draconians had long been pirates of the universe, pillaging celestial bodies to gain control over them to drain them of their life energy. The Atlantians did their best to curb this behavior and were forced to constantly engage the Draconians.

As the Draconians used some, but not all Atlantian technology, it created stalemate conditions in various areas of conflict. The Atlantians were at least able to provide enough protection to our earth and humans as a species by driving the Draconians underground and holding them in a kind of limbo in the earth's subterranean surface layer by harnessing the resonance of the earth's natural frequency as the Draconian's own prison.

The earth's frequency was the only thing protecting them and they knew it so they used their own form of negative frequency manipulation to manipulate men into giving them the resources that they wanted by means of indirect control. We have been held hostage and used as guinea pigs and food for the Draconian captors who were captive because of their own greed and volition. It was an endless game of chess where humans were the pawns constantly in check.

The Draconians needed to release their mind controlling hold over humanity as the only Atlantian condition on freeing them from their subterranean lair. The Atlantians did not force this action because it would have triggered the immediate dissolution of all life on the planet due to the frequency hold the Draconians had wielded over us since our beginning; a failsafe deterrent inherent in the technology they were using.

This deadlock that had been building for ages was a cancer that had encroached on every living thing to varying degrees and needed to be rooted out before humanity passed its own event horizon and destroyed itself.

As I moved, I was searching for Candace, but all I could find was an empty space in the present dimension. I could see her and sense her in the past and in endless variations of dimensions, I knew she was still here, but she was hidden somehow. I went to be with her in a different dimension when she was searching for me, just to see her face again. I listened to her heart as it hung in anticipation in hopes of finding me.

I admired Danny for what he had done to help her and remembered his face and voice from the day of the last riot. There was good in them both, their intentions were pure. I saw them get arrested and where they were taken to be held, but then they both disappeared behind a deep disturbance that was shielding them from me.

There were very few spots on the planet that were absolute dead zones to my perception, like spikes of distorted frequencies that blocked out everything to me, this was one of those places and it was deep beneath NanoCell's corporate headquarters.

Their building housed the research and development division as well as the main laboratory for the global titan whose annual revenue literally approaches a quadrillion dollars annually due to their advancements in commercializing over the counter cell-rejuvenative treatments for every kind of ailment from the common cold to stage 4 cancers.

Their methods of implementing this kind of technology were so advanced that they could repair any disease in the body, but also leave trace elements that analyze, replicate and remain stored in the body. The nano-sized trace elements the medication left behind were ready to cause the nervous system and brain activity to slow until they come to a crawl if the patient stopped taking the medication.

The patient would live a long and "healthy" life free of common past ailments, but only as long as they kept taking the medication. Those who stopped taking the medication succumbed to deterioration of the body, synthesizing rapid aging and resulting in vastly reduced lifespans due to the reintroduction of the disease into the patient's body. They had created the perfect dependency, the ultimate drug they marketed as the fountain of youth. There was never a more deceiving mask as the one the corporate agenda was wearing as they welcomed the world to their most elaborate and profitable masquerade.

They had a pill for everything that was slowly bleeding the life and wealth out of every living thing on the planet. The medication was derived from information given to them by the Draconians, it also helped keep humans more docile and readily controlled for experiments they performed on humans.

Everything was very well planned, manipulated and watched by the Draconians by exploiting the easily appeased and controlled ruling "elite." These elite had used tax money to secretly build hundreds of underground bases that housed hundreds or even thousands of Draconians in each, depending on the size of the Draconian hive in that area. The elite even held fundraisers the 99% called wars every few years in which they catered to and profited from both sides of the "opposition."

The earth's crust was the Draconian prison and haven. They were like hives all over the world, deep underground. The sprawling network of tunnels that connected top secret places all over the world were endless; they were all connected through one tunnel or another. The Draconians and their human subservients could shuttle anywhere in the world in complete secrecy and safety in a matter of minutes giving them an obvious strategic and logistical advantage in any situation they wanted to exploit in the past. It had been abused to no end over time and kept things neatly in their favor.

I had seen the physical subterranean networks in the earth, the network of a person's life long interpersonal connections, what they stemmed from and where they grew and how the poisonous roots were growing so densely around the human race that it had become a race to stop it from choking itself. We had allowed weeds to grow in our garden by remaining idle and negligent. The intentions of the connections were crystal clear.

I wanted to engage Conrad to give him an ultimatum, without causing a public scare so I decided to go to the darkest place justice still dared to exist. I stopped by the library to go fishing for hacktivist royalty with a short public video I posted to 4chan that said

"0dys3us has fallen in defense of a fearless woman on her quest to bring the light of life and freedom to our world, will you cast a shadow or remain in them?"

I had signed the post with only an email address to a temporary account I set up and the responses came flooding in within minutes from Danny's friends and colleagues from all over the world offering their technical services and expertise, which was exactly what I was hoping for. One email in particular caught my eye right away. It indicated that efforts were being coordinated as I read by someone who called themselves "SParrow" who claimed to have worked closely with 0dys3us over the years and spoke with a lot of respect toward Danny. I searched him out and quickly confirmed his identity and the intent of his heart; it was all I needed to know that I had at least one ally.

I replied to SParrow thanking him for his efforts and let him know I was standing by for any specifics he was offering. Several minutes passed but soon there was an update.

"Initial probes into infiltrating NanoCell's datacloud have failed. We have successfully defeated their encryption element in the past, but those methods are no longer effective as

171

the NanoCell network seems to retract no matter what we attempt. Speaking of clouds, there are global storm clouds gathering. Anonymous grows in strength like dataclouds when the cause arises and justice is demanded. A distress call has been put out to the major siteops to coordinate the reconnaissance and implementation when we are ready. All siteops have been responding affirmatively and dedicating resources toward the search…"

I was pleasantly surprised at the speed at which he was spearheading this. There were many that were eager to take a stand against the corporate tyrants, they just usually lacked direction and non-disinformation. I replied

"Thank you very much for all of your efforts - Asher"

I got an immediate reply back from SParrow requesting to chat which I accepted.

SParrow: As in Asher Wry?!

Asher: yes

SParrow: holy crap, we thought you were dead, everybody did, what happened?

Asher: it's a long story, tell ya later ;)

Asher: right now what's important is getting danny and candace back

SParrow: who's this candace chick anyway, she better be hot, lulz

Asher: candace vanderbilt

SParrow: what?! the daughter of conrad vanderbilt? why would we do that? we'll help you get danny out, but you're on your own with her, she's the enemy's spawn!

Asher: listen, danny is a stand-up guy, he wouldn't be with her if she was any kind of threat

SParrow: she's the reason he's locked up right now!

Asher: i understand how you must feel about her, but she is not like her father, i know her heart.

SParrow: dood, calm down, you don't need to wax-poetic here, i was just trolling you man. of course, if danny trusts her that's good enough for me. it's good to talk to a fellow patriot

Asher: brothers in arms

SParrow: ok, I'll keep you posted, over and out

SParrow's quick wit made me smile; I could sense his enthusiasm and determination as he continued working to find a way to access NanoCell.

With that in motion, I directed my attention to Conrad Vanderbilt. It did not take long before rumors of me *not* being detained or dead started circulating online, so I knew it wouldn't be long before Conrad was aware of that fact as well.

The library was quietly deceiving. People raged internally all around me in spite of their outward demeanor of silence. There were so many different people from different cultures

173

and backgrounds, asking the same questions and facing the same struggles. The one thing that I saw again and again that these people had in common, despite their differences was hope.

Hope for inner peace, hope for love and a global unity in a spiritual sense, not governmentally. Hope is the most human of emotions and one that is shared by no other species. Hope is a defining, uniting singularity that everyone can understand and champion. Seeing that there was still good in people gave *me* hope. It justified the cause and became the plane on which we operated. Candace had kept hope alive for me; it was what was driving her before she disappeared. That alone was a quality worth fighting for.

Just then, I felt a slight nudge followed by a thud and the subsequent crying of a small child. I turned around in my chair to see a boy, no older than four who had tripped on the foot of my chair. I bent over to lift him up and he immediately stopped crying. He looked at me quizzically and asked

"Why are your eyes so shiny?"

"They're just reflecting the light."

I said. His mother was quick to retrieve him from me and thanked me in spite of the distrust I sensed from her. The boy posed the same question about my eyes to his flustered mother. The woman glanced at me and tersely told him

"they're just eyes, just like ours Michael." The woman scooped the boy up and held him on her hip as she walked away. The boy faced me as she left with him. He yelled out again this time

"look mom, they're shiny, see?"

The woman did not look back and quickened her pace instead; I smiled at him as they walked away. He was able to see something his mother was oblivious to. I was able to see only light in the boy while his mother had many dark spots inside her, signs of her intent. He was uncompromised innocence in true form.

As they left, I turned back to the computer where I had another email waiting from SParrow that read:

"Asher, if we can't get to NanoCell directly, we can get to them indirectly. We have identified 37 of NanoCell's subsidiaries and strategic partners as targets that will definitely get their attention. We are currently preparing a strike against NanoCell's distributors, marketing agencies, suppliers and financial partners in an aggressive DDoS attack that will bring their networks to their knees. We should be prepared to strike within the hour. ~SParrow"

This sounded like a start, or at least a distraction for the time being, but I had

175

something else in mind first. I immediately responded back to SParrow saying:

"Thank you for that lightning-fast coordinated effort SParrow, but I think we need to make a preemptive statement before we flex that kind of muscle. I have seen some of your video statements in the past, taking a stand on different issues and I think this is a prime opportunity that we can't miss to make sure the public knows exactly what and who NanoCell is and why they should care. Can you present this text in the same disguised-voice message format that Anonymous is famous for? ;) Any kind of pictures or video clips to enhance the video message would be a bonus, but the Anonymous logo is just fine since we're in a time crunch.

Citizens of the world, as you are no doubt familiar with the global conglomerate NanoCell, we need to make you more fully aware of some of their more nefarious undertakings. For decades now, NanoCell has been the largest pharmaceutical company in the world providing their mind and body altering wonder drugs to cure everything from the common cold to reversing the effects of final stage cancers.

Unfortunately as many of you have experienced with a loved one, once their drugs are taken, the regiment cannot be stopped or the disease returns with more ferocity and abandon than it originally had. The technology used in NanoCell's drugs behaves in such a way as to place blame on the original disease, but the devil is in the details. The drug does actually destroy the disease in the body, but before it does, the nano particles scan, replicate and reproduce the disease and store it dormantly inside the host gathering in the brain and in the heart.

When the nano-particles no longer receive the expected dose of NanoCell's drugs through the bloodstream, they aggressively start to multiply their dormant copies they stored when the drug was first taken and aggressively redistribute the disease again throughout the victim's body. The drugs first install themselves and then wait for the consistent subsequent flow of drugs; when we stop paying, we get shut off just like the utility companies.

Those unfortunate enough to have taken NanoCell drugs are paying rent to keep themselves alive after unknowingly signing over the deed to their bodies. The diseases we as humans are susceptible to have been mass produced by the corporate world and injected into every single aspect of human life for thousands of years and have been dramatically accelerated over the past 100 years.

Make no mistake, NanoCell and the vast majority of corporate scum have zero regard for any human life. They aim to filter out the 99% that they deem inferior and to gather as much control and resources as they possibly can as we fall dead beneath their feet.

Why would they want to kill 99% of the world's population you may ask yourself, who would produce the goods and services they need then? They are playing the odds. They would even settle for eliminating even 80% of human life, it would make the remainder much easier to control and exploit compared to the over-population problem they feel they have today. They want to cut us down to a manageable size so we don't keep destroying what they feel is their world.

The ruling elite is a group of 12 men who sit at the top of all global corporate activity and thus government activity. One of those men is Conrad Vanderbilt, head of the NanoCell corporation. Those 12 men are in turn controlled by three hidden masters who are the intermediaries between the 12 and an ancient alien race called the Draconians who have been ruling over humans and this world since the dawn of man. There is no end that they will not seek to get what they want. We are diseased livestock to the Draconians and their subservient corporations and governments.

NanoCell is currently holding two hostages and we are calling for their immediate release, Danny Roberts and Candace Vanderbilt, Conrad Vanderbilt's own daughter. This information was never meant to be public as it would obviously interrupt their end game objectives.

We the people will not stand by and take this information lying down. We will fight until our dying breath, not only for basic human rights, but to maintain the moral fiber we rely on as humans to sustain our souls and keep our agency free. There is no greater cause and there has never been more of a threat to our existence than that which we are facing now. If the two hostages are not safely released and NanoCell's activities ceased within the next 24 hours, there will be dire consequences.

Will you cast a shadow or remain in them?"

I hit send and waited for a few minutes. SParrow did not take long before he replied

"whoaaaa man, that is seriously heavy, I'm going to run this by the siteops to get the consensus, I'll talk to you soon."

I sat in silent meditation for several minutes in the aether's current, aligning myself with the light. I refocused myself when SParrow's response came back saying

"It was nearly unanimous; there are only a few besides me who believe any of this. Corrupt corporations and government are one thing that people are willing to stand up against, but "fictionalized stories with little to back them up is a completely different ball game, where is the proof?" is the general sentiment being discussed over IRC chat. Without anything to back up that outlandish story, I don't think you're going to get many takers. To be honest, I'm not sure I can get on board with it either."

After reading this, I stood up and slipped from the library into the warehouse-type loft I could see SParrow and his friend Andy were working out of in San Francisco. SParrow and his friend both had extensive workstations littered with cables, peripherals, empty pizza boxes and empty energy drink cans. Each workstation was kiddy corner facing each other in the sparsely decorated space with heavy drapes blocking out most of the sunlight.

Neither of them noticed me appear in the room, because of the pounding industrial music and low light. I raised my hand and suppressed the sound of their speakers to get their attention, but this only caused SParrow to pay more attention to the music player on his computer trying to fix what he thought had gone wrong with the sound.

"SParrow"

I called out. A scruffy beard and wide eyes framed in Buddy Holly glasses shot out from behind his three matching monitors.

"Or do you prefer Jay, face to face?"

I said

"*Who* are you and *how* did you get in here?" he demanded.

"It's Asher, we were just talking, I just figured it would be more believable this way."

I heard the unmistakable mechanics of a shotgun cocking behind me. I raised my hands in a peaceful offering to show them I meant no harm and turned to look at his friend.

"It's ok Andy, really."

Andy's wiry body barely looked like it could manage holding the weapon. I turned to look at Jay again

"Sorry, I don't believe you, I traced that IP and it was a public library in New York, try again. How do you know our names? Who are you working for? This is private property and if you don't start answering now, we're well within our rights to dispatch you."

I turned again to look at Andy who was stoically still, still pointing a sawed-off shotgun squarely at my head.

"None of the alarms were set off and none of the security monitors have detected anything all day."

"Who are you and how did you get in here!"

Andy yelled, he had a shaky urgency in his voice that made him sound unstable, which made me a bit uneasy that he was the one with the gun. The situation was escalated too quickly and I needed to re-approach them.

I slipped out of the loft again, disappearing for a few seconds. I reappeared behind Andy, easily taking the gun from his hands. I threw the gun up in the air and into the ceiling where it disappeared like a stone in water; I had their full attention now.

"Can we talk guys? How else would I know how to pick up our email conversation, let alone appear here if I wasn't Asher? I'm asking for your help, for me, for Danny, for Candace and for everyone."

I motioned for them to both come out from behind their desks they were nearly cowering behind at this point to sit on the couch against the other corner of the loft. They both walked over slowly and sat on opposite sides of the broken in couch. I pulled up a chair in front of them so we could all talk at eye level.

"If you can do all that disappearing and magic stuff, why would you need our help?"

Jay said snidely. Andy was busy wiping sweat from his palms on his pants.

"Everyone has limits. I can't exactly explain it, but I've seen things and been places that I never could have dreamed of a few months ago. I didn't ask for it, but it was given to me and it's a responsibility that I intend to sentry. You need to understand and trust me that this isn't a game. Understand that this is life or death, for everybody. There are only a few places on earth that I cannot get to or see. They are protected by the same source of alien technology that empowers me. The NanoCell facility under their corporate headquarters is one of those places. It's deep underground and completely unknown to the world except for the few humans that are cleared to work there. NanoCell's technology is a direct result of their interaction and collaboration with the Draconians who stole technology from the

Atlantians aeons ago. Is there anything else you'd like to ask or do you need a demonstration?"

I was terse at this point from trying to drive the point home to them. Andy just shook his head nervously and Jay also declined quickly.

"This is just a distraction, to send a message to NanoCell and Conrad that we are serious; the world is about to turn against them. What do you say guys; are we gonna do this?"

"Come on"

Jay said to Andy and they both quickly walked back to their work stations and began working feverishly to get the plan back on track. I followed Jay back and stood next to and behind him as he worked. He got back on IRC and announced that the video is going forward.

"I just got a very unexpected visit from Asher and can personally vouch for this message, this is real, we *need* to make this happen, yesterday!"

He continued chatting with a few other people who were on board. Apparently he had quite a strong pull in the Anonymous community and respected as one of the few actual hackers that could pull off coordinating and more importantly implementing deep level programming hacks. He was among the elite group that the vast majority of Anonymous supporters followed by pointing their LOIC's to take down network and server targets when the need and cause arose, which was the virtual equivalent of an old fashioned peaceful occupation.

There was a tremendous amount of activity happening with different members of his small group whom were reporting info from their own smaller groups and culling the information for the video in the form of regular updates that were ultimately approved by Jay and I as they would come in. The video was being put together by people all over the world, bit by bit and at an alarming rate. Once we approved material, it was put in the cloud from which the actual video editor was able to draw from. It felt like I was watching a time-lapse ant farm video.

Within ten minutes all the content was delivered to an editor in Slovenia that layered in the rendered computer voice behind all the images in sequence to flow with the message. And less than a half hour later we were viewing the completed video edit on Jay's machine; it was a perfectly flowing and cohesive video. Jay looked at me as the last frame played as if to ask if it was ready to go out. I nodded and Jay uploaded it making it live.

We watched it begin to go viral over the next hour and waited for what would happen in response, from the public and from

NanoCell. As expected, there was mounting pressure building online in public opinion, but no word from NanoCell. Reports began to surface on various independent news outlets breaking the story and it started getting pretty heavily shared through social media, but the story had not gained any mainstream traction yet. The story was getting more negative attention than anything, believed by some, but mocked by most.

About three hours after the video was posted, the mainstream media outlets erupted. Major news outlets started spewing breaking news that a bomb had exploded at a major NanoCell distribution hub just outside of Philadelphia. Initial reports indicated dozens of critical injuries and had confirmed three dead with that number expected to rise as more information was learned.

This was obviously horrific and to make matters worse, the media had placed the blame squarely on the shoulders of Asher Wry & Anonymous; we were all being setup by this false flag attack. The news reports went on to confirm this information was coming from a number of federal agencies who had now named myself and Anonymous the only suspects.

It light of these new events, we went to work, shifting our original focus from mounting a cyber-attack on NanoCell's surrounding companies to the media itself in hopes of minimizing the collateral damage. Anonymous had always had an unspoken rule not to attack the media as they believed in free speech as a basic human right, it's one of the founding principles that allowed their voice, but all bets were off now, if they wanted a war, they definitely asked for it.

"Time to call in the troops?"

Andy asked from across the room.

"The troops, the reserves and the veterans."

Jay called back. Andy smiled, cracked his knuckles and began typing up a storm. Jay pushed up his glasses, furrowed his brow and let loose on the keyboard. Andy sent out a battle cry to everyone calling for the immediate takedown of the mainstream media giants that were propagating the false accusations. Sadly, the human suffering was real; NanoCell had gone so far as to deliberately bomb its own facilities, killing and maiming many of its own employees to send a message that they would not be challenged, just as they had done endless times before in more traditional clandestine forms.

Jay went to work on a deeper interruption to the media infrastructure, trying to hack their systems and installing backdoor software to help keep them down and from implementing workarounds. While they were working, the situation only worsened. The death toll of those killed in the blast had risen to 24 as emergency crews extinguished the burning wreckage of the massive distribution center and first responders continued to pull people from building.

Within the hour, an emergency press conference was underway by officials of the Pennsylvania governor's office stating that they had been working with state and local law enforcement as well as the FBI and CIA, confirming that key individuals affiliated with Anonymous were in fact responsible for the attack, but only I was specifically named as coordinating the attack.

They further confirmed that they had uncovered a much more sinister plan. They referenced a second video supposedly released by Anonymous which was a complete hoax, intended to look, sound and feel like it had come from Anonymous. The video stated that I was coordinating something much worse with Anonymous and was prepared to detonate 25 biological weapons, supposedly obtained from nefarious Anonymous connections, in major international cities since there had been no attempt by NanoCell to contact Anonymous or cease their operations.

The press conference concluded by stating that warrants for my immediate arrest had been issued and that they were seeking "persons of interest within the Anonymous community." Our video made Anonymous and I the perfect villain and scapegoats they were looking for to fire back. Their video made things horribly serious by completely flipping the tables on us. The rabbit hole kept getting deeper, but neither I nor Anonymous was about to take that lying down.

After about an hour Jay and Andy both confirmed that there was now enough support in place to proceed with the takedown. I gave the go ahead and within minutes all the major network news outlets went silent. I could feel the energy behind the gathering force, Anonymous was not a force to be taken lightly. Their power and numbers increased steadily, holding the frontline of media attacks back with full force. Even with Jay's backdoor software, it was only a matter of time before it would be defeated; maybe hours, maybe days, but the clock was ticking.

The darkness I saw encroaching on our world was growing and spreading interdimentionally as I looked ahead through the aeons of aether. There was still no opening around the underground NanoCell lab where Candace and Danny were being held and I could only hope that they were still alive somewhere inside.

"I appreciate everything you guys have done to help."

Andy and Jay both looked up, but neither of them said anything, they just tightened their mouths from a concentrated frown into a straightened kind of half smile.

"I need to go deal with a few things, I'll be back soon if I can. Anything you can do to digitally demoralize and contain the media, NanoCell or their network will help, thanks again guys"

I said.

"Don't worry, we'll get 'em"

Jay said, barely glancing away from his screens and with that I slipped out of the loft.

Ch. 8
| wisdom |

I slipped from the loft into a sphere under the pond in Central Park where I had been with Candace before. I needed to contact Vasha; I needed help. I could sense her still, inside me in a way, but in trying to sync with her, there was no response, no dial tone, just dead air on the line. What I was feeling was just my feeling of a connection with her inside myself, not the open reciprocation we had in inner earth. I felt cut off and alone, like an unanswered prayer.

I couldn't feel the beings of light either, like they were behind some sort of veil like the NanoCell facility and the handful of other dead spots on earth. I could however feel the pulse of the earth's heart that I could not feel before. It was vibrant and unmistakable as my heart synced with its rhythm. My heart rate was completely unwavering and it beat with cosmic force inside my body. It was pulsing in sync with my heart. I concentrated and communicated what I felt to the heart of the earth in hopes of using it as a way to communicate what I needed.

The veil was kept in place by the same Atlantian technology that the Draconians stole and were using to help NanoCell hide their facilities. The Atlantians must have known this. I didn't understand why they would have chosen me or allowed me to have this power and then shut me out; this was the time I needed them most. I had knowledge of the universe, I could travel interdimentionally and to any point in time I wanted, but I was at a complete impasse with this eternal dead end.

I closed my eyes and lost myself in a moment Candace and I had shared. She was pure light and she radiated within me.

I opened my eyes and slipped out the sphere and onto the street. I could see by now, TV coverage displayed on a screen as I passed by a cafe across from the NanoCell building. The hack hadn't lasted long. I sensed the hair on the back of a woman's neck stand up as she listened to the news reports.

The air was getting thicker with tension although you wouldn't know it by the general street demeanor. I crossed the street onto the NanoCell grounds. I kept a casual pace in spite of the growing resistance I felt the closer I got to the building entrance. It felt like trying to push magnetic opposites together combined with a deep sea pressure compression on every square inch of my body.

I reached out for the lobby door to open it and could not even place my hand on the handle. The force was so strong at this point that it was an impenetrable barrier around the entire building. The shied was a wall of emptiness to my soul. There was nothing else like it in the universe I could sense. It was the absence of absence, a great abyss lacking even nothing. There was no visual or physical indication that anything was different at all about the building. Then it was just gone, the world beyond the shield continued; I could immediately sense everything and everyone inside the building.

The immensity of the building was astonishing; it was like an expansive ant farm. A labyrinth of hallways and rooms spread out over 24 underground levels were secretly connected to the skyscraper above.

Candace was here, I could feel her light again within me and the sadness she felt. She was surrounded by dark energy. She and Danny were deep underground on the nineteenth level. Conrad and a heavily staffed security team were hidden away on the second underground floor beneath the parking levels in a fortified command center. He was controlling the building's shield from there.

I immediately slipped into the room Candace was being held in. I found her sitting in the corner of the cold bright room, hugging her legs and resting her chin on her knees.

"Asher!"

She screamed as she jumped up and ran toward me, slamming into me like a linebacker. We fit together like puzzle pieces and held each other hard as we became one again. I felt her heart sync with mine as it joined the rhythmic harmony of mine with the inner suns. I synced to her and she understood. It startled her severely, but she was quickly at ease again.

"I missed you so much, I didn't know if I'd ever feel you again. I don't know how much time we have, but we need to go. Your father is watching us from security. Anonymous and I have been setup. He bombed his own building and is now threatening to frame us again by waging international biological warfare on the world. Less than one percent of the population of the world could afford the antidote they have prepared after these bombs begin to propagate their infection."

I could feel the horror build in her mind as I synced this. I showed her countless thousands, sick and dying with red rings around their eyes.

"What happening Asher? What are we going to do? We need to save Danny if he's here, he helped me, he can help us."

She spoke in a quick and clearly shaken voice.

"He's here."

I said. Still gripping tightly to me, we both slipped out of her cell and into Danny's.

"Danny, let's go, we're leaving"

I said quickly. He was lying on the floor of the small room and jolted from the laying position, backing away with his hands and feet until he hit the wall. He moved fairy quickly for still being on his back and the condition he was in.

"Relax, no one's here to hurt you."

I motioned with my hand still extended to him, trying to ease his traumatized mind. He acted like a rescue animal. He had been severely beaten during several interrogation sessions he had endured. His body was bruised and cut like the landscape of a battleground.

Candace and I both extended a hand to him which he reluctantly took. We raised his broken body up carefully. I could feel his pain shooting through his body; the pain compounded the more vertical he became. It was nearly unbearable for him but he was able to stand and walk on his own.

"How did you get here?"

Danny's dusty voice sounded strained like he was in a haze.

"We'll explain it to you later, right now we need to get out of here."

Just as I finished saying that, the shield around the NanoCell building was up again and I could see nothing on the outside. I could sense BlackCorp security teams starting to mobilize throughout the building.

"I need you both to do something"

"Anything"

Candace replied.

"I need you to get in touch with Anonymous again; they need your help Danny. We need to get media control. SParrow will bring you up to speed on the technical side of things. You're just going to have to trust me on this one. We need to mass broadcast a message of love to the world. Candace, the world needs you, they need to see your light; they need to feel what I've felt. Share your light with them."

"But I have no idea what to say, I don't have a message"

she said.

"When the time comes you'll know what to say, it will come to you."

I smiled at them both and slipped the three of us out of the underground room and into the lobby of the building where we couldn't go any further. We appeared in the NanoCell lobby and were far from alone.

~

Danny and I turned in time to see Asher seizing on the floor. He had been hit by some kind of energy beams by several of the BlackCorp operatives. He was having extreme difficulty breathing and his skin was sucked tight against his bones and muscles; he looked like he was going to implode.

"Noooo, you're killing him!"

I screamed so loud my throat hurt. The lobby was crawling with BlackCorp operatives all armed to the teeth with extremely high tech weapons and protective gear I'd never seen before. Just like that, the brilliant light connecting Asher and I was gone again, replaced by a black wall of noise inside my head.

"Going somewhere?"

I cringed at the all too familiar condescending voice that echoed through the cavernous lobby. My father made his way through the poised operatives who were all awaiting their next order from him.

"So rude to leave without saying goodbye Candace, I would expect that from these two, but not from you sweetie."

He raised his hand to shoulder height and motioned with two fingers. As he casually strolled over to the center of the lobby where we were, four of the operatives ran over and were restraining Danny and I before my father reached us. Asher was still totally

196

incapacitated in a twisted fetal position. I could feel my blood start to boil just looking at his smug face.

"Let us go!"

I screamed at the two men that had grabbed me on each of my sides. Danny was in no condition to resist, futile as it was. I couldn't fight back the tears that began rolling down my face.

"Why are you doing this?"

I pleaded.

"Don't flatter yourself, this isn't about you, it never was."

My father was pacing, circling around us. He pushed Asher over onto his back with an aggressive heel to his shoulder

"This young man has something that belongs to me."

He ripped open Asher's shirt to inspect his chest expecting to find the starskin, but there was nothing there.

"Where is it?"

His voice exploded with an animalistic rage that rang out for several seconds in the cavernous lobby. I was relieved for a moment when there was no sign of it. He stared at us all in disgust then composed himself after a few moments, his nostrils flaring from heavily distraught breathing. His face slowly cracked into a disturbed smile.

"No matter."

He said. Something in his brain flipped and his personality changed. He now exuded a creepy, gleefully dark glow like a sixties game show host in a wax museum. He began pacing around us even slower than before and stopped behind us. He reached up and started petting our heads in a synchronous motion like two cats. His hands slid down our heads and necks.

I felt an acute stabbing pain shoot through every nerve in my body as he ripped out a white staple-shaped tube that had been feeding us regular doses of some kind of strange drugs. He dropped them both on the ground behind us and began laughing. Neither of us could stand for a minute, but the operatives that were restraining us kept us held in place like shirts on hangers, in fact they anticipated it.

He started walking around again to face us. He looked at us with a sideways smirk and shrugged.

"Those are company property, inventory control, you understand. Well, I got everything that belonged to me back so I think that should about do it, you're free to go."

His countenance was completely refreshed; he was smiling and spoke with an extremely upbeat tone now as if a massive weight had been lifted off his shoulders. It was a new level of disturbing, even for my callous father. He raised his eyebrows and said

"See them out would you?"

to the operatives that were holding us. They started marching us to the lobby doors.

"Give our friend here another dose while the shield is down, for insurance purposes."

I jerked my head around sharply in time to see three other operatives pummeling energy beams into Asher's poor body, still shutdown from the first assault. I was kicking and dragging my feet trying to stop the advance to the doors, but it was a useless effort. I was sobbing and screaming uncontrollably.

"No, no, no, please no, Asher!"

I heard the doors unlock just before we reached them and we were literally thrown out. The doors locked again and I scrambled to my feet and ran back to grab the door handle, but I couldn't even get to the handle to touch it. The shield had been activated in addition to the physical locks.

I watched helplessly as they dragged Asher's lifeless body across the cold polished marble into the elevator. I had never cried so hysterically. Danny pleaded with me.

"Candace, we need to go, now!"

"Then go! I'm not going anywhere"

I snapped back at him and fell to my knees in pain from reacting so severely. The pain in my neck was getting warm and there was a dull tingling feeling aching in my nerves.

"Listen, I know you don't want to leave him, but we can't do anything from here, not right now"

Danny became more sympathetic seeing my reaction.

"You don't know anything."

I said. The concrete beneath me was beginning to pool with tears.

"You're right, I don't understand, but understand that I am going to do everything I can to help you. If there is a way we'll find it."

His words were no consolation, but I realized my options were few and far between at this point. He held out his hand to help me up, it was covered in defensive lacerations. I looked to the pooling tears in defeat and stubbornly took it.

"Come on"

he said. He was trying to keep composed through the intense pain he must have been feeling as he helped me up.

Ch. 9
| insight |

Danny and I headed out through the pavilion and onto the street, quickly trying to create as much distance as possible between us and NanoCell. We were still dressed in our white jumpsuits that we had been given while imprisoned, but no one gave us a second look. Everyone seemed to be in a bigger hurry than usual today.

We were toward midtown, looking for anywhere we could duck out and get internet access for Danny to get connected again. We kept walking for a while until we reached the library at Chatham Square. Since neither of us had a library card, we did our best to distract a pre-teen boy who was busy wasting time online by telling him the library was giving out free cookies on the other side of the library which he took hook, line and sinker.

Danny quickly got setup, easily bypassing the limiting safeguards on the public computer. I felt a small level of paranoia and kept watch as he worked his magic. He started chatting with his fellow anons on a secure channel. People were very surprised and excited to see him back and in his element.

Danny was typing ridiculously fast and the chat window kept moving with a positive and steady cadence. He was saying hello, taking jabs at old friends to break the ice again and getting his fair share of trolling as well. He didn't keep this up for long at all before shifting to a more serious tone.

They all started discussing the recent events of the past day. SParrow chimed in and caught him up with what he and Andy were doing with Asher and what had been set in motion so far. Danny explained how the plans had changed.

"We still need to gain control of the media's satellite network and keep it this time, but for a different purpose. Asher has asked Candace to broadcast an important message to the world and that's what we need to help make happen. We were just with Asher in New York and were forced to leave, we had no choice. Conrad Vanderbilt is torturing Asher right now at NanoCell, or worse; we're lucky to be here and alive at all. I'm with Candace right now. Asher saved our lives by trading himself for our freedom. He sacrificed himself for us. I don't know any more than that. All I know is that whatever he has planned, I'm going to help him do this. Who's with me?"

There was overwhelming response of support from everyone on the channel.

"One immediate concern is that we're at a library now and are in need of a safe house with a fast link."

Most of the offers were generous, but too far away from where we were. A message came over from someone calling himself dev/lulz saying he would be willing to help us, and he was close.

"Do you know him?"

I asked Danny.

"No, not really, I mean I've seen him around on this channel, but he's pretty quiet for the most part and has only ever done some low level stuff as far as I know."

He said. I didn't have a good feeling about it

"Is it safe? This sounds pretty sketchy."

"I don't know, but we don't have much to lose at this point"

He said. He was snappy, but I chalked it up to his pain. If he felt anything like I did, it couldn't be good. I was doing my best to keep from showing the pain I was in; I didn't want him to think I was more of a liability than I was already feeling. I felt like this was all my fault. If I hadn't taken Asher to see my father's collection, if I hadn't gotten him involved in my world, he wouldn't have had to trade himself for our freedom. The guilt was unbearable and made me feel dark and ugly inside.

Danny got dev/lulz's address and scrawled it on a scrap of paper, it was only a few blocks away in Chinatown. Danny stood up and we looked at each other for a few seconds as if to ask if we were both sure that we wanted to do this. I could feel we were both a bit apprehensive, but with no objections he said

"Lets go."

He was solemn as he almost whispered it under his breath. We noticed our white jumpsuits were a bit more obvious in the quiet library. People were whispering and looking in our direction. We walked as quickly as we could to the exit, trying not to draw any unnecessary attention.

Out on the street, there was more whispering. People were taking a lot more notice than they were earlier. I don't know if we were just more paranoid or if it was the fact that we were heading into Chinatown, the heart of organized crime for the past three decades. The urge to get to our safe house was gaining momentum with every unsure step. We ignored the looks and talking in our direction until we came to the address.

We found ourselves standing in front of a Chinese market that smelled like the cooling had broken, but continued to operate despite triple digit temperatures.

The old brick building had apartments above the street level businesses. We started up the stairs on our way to the fourth floor. The pungent stench grew stronger with every step we took up; the building was getting hotter the higher we went. It felt much hotter here than outside by the time we found ourselves standing in from of the beat up old door bearing the numbers "417."

Danny knocked quietly at first; it seemed everything he did was cautious and stealth, it was just his nature. I had no idea what to expect, but I was genuinely scared at what we might find on the other side of the door. We saw the peephole go dark as the stranger on the other side got to assess *us* first. The five or six locks and latches rattled through the door like a machine and the door swung open.

"Odyseus, come in" the man said excitedly. He was heavyset and seemed enthusiastic to have company. It was fairly dark inside, but lit well enough to walk.

"Follow me"

he said. We both looked at each other reluctantly, but feeling it was too late to turn back now if we wanted to have a chance at making this happen, we had to go deeper into the unknown. We walked down a long hall that was barely wide enough for the heavyset man to walk down due to white filing boxes on either side of the hall that were all marked by individual months and years. The boxes were stacked to the ceiling all the way down the hall. He was a hoarder of some kind, but at least he was organized about it.

We got to the end of the hall and followed him into a room that was a bit brighter, due to a surprising amount of light that was being emitted from the racks and racks of servers and loudly humming computer equipment in the room. The room was much cooler than the rest of the building because of an industrial sized air conditioning unit that felt like an arctic wind rushing through everything in the room; no doubt to keep all of the equipment at an optimal temperature. It was even more elaborate than Danny's setup.

He grabbed a couple of folding chairs from a closet just outside of the room and set them up behind and flanking his chair. There was barely enough room to sit down behind his throne like office chair.

"Please, sit"

He said. He was very polite in spite of his awkward motions. He sat down and turned around to face us. He was shy toward me and could barely make eye contact. He was poised toward Danny

"Thank you for coming Odyseus, it's an honor"

he said.

"Please, call me Danny and thank you for helping us out, we'd be in big trouble without your help."

206

He seemed a little let down that Danny didn't want to go by his screen name.

"Yes, thank you very much"

I added, smiling at him graciously.

"Forgive me, but I always feel weird calling people by their screen names."

Danny said.

"Fair enough, an eye for an eye, my name's Bryan, we'll keep it at that"

He said.

"Fair enough"

Danny replied with a chuckle.

"So, hacking the media's network of satellites huh? I like it, straight for the jugular."

Bryan said. His voice was higher pitched that I would have guessed for a man of his size, almost cartoon like. He wasn't tall, but was probably pushing about 300 pounds. He was jovial, yet spoke very matter-of-factly.

Danny and Bryan started in on a long technical conversation about how they planned on hacking the satellite network; I understood almost none of their technical jargon. I was at ease though as they were both extremely confident, almost bragging and trying to one up each other. They were both bouncing ideas off each other and building their strategy as if they had been working as a team for years. In a sense, they had. It was really amazing to watch them spark new ideas in each other. Their faces lit up like kids on Christmas morning when they would finish each other's sentences.

As exciting as this bro-bonding was, it was frequently interrupted by searing pains that waved down from my neck and shot through my spine into the rest of my body.

"Sssssss"

I inhaled quickly as the pain hit again. I reached up to hold my neck to try to calm my nerves and ease the pain. They both stopped mid-sentence and looked at me.

"Are you ok?"

Bryan said. He seemed a bit annoyed at first glance, then turned to concern when he saw me cringing in pain. I was grinding my teeth with my eyes closed tight. Danny put his arm on my shoulder

"Candace, are you ok?"

Danny had more genuine concern in his voice as he was likely experiencing the same pain, but it didn't make it feel any better.

"Fine... I'm ok"

I eked out between breaths after a few moments. The stabbing pain throbbed all through my body in sync with the beat of my heart and was fading slowly with each pump. I breathed deeply as the pain subsided trying to help it along its course. I pulled my hand down away from my neck to rest it on my lap.

"Candace?"

Danny's spoke gravely now. He grabbed my wrist and turned my hand over so it was visible to all of us. My fingers were smeared with blood. Seeing the blood scared me, starting an involuntary trembling motion in my arm. Bryan reached for a package of wet wipes that was sitting next to his monitors and handed them to Danny to help me. He seemed really freaked out by the sight of blood.

"What's going on here?"

Bryan demanded.

"Danny put his arm around me and explained to Bryan where we had just been and the backstory of why all this was happening which slowly diffused him and helped him grasp exactly what we were doing and why we were in this situation that led us to him.

"Everything happens for a reason you know"

Bryan said confidently. The look on his face told me he felt proud and destined to be a part of this. Bryan turned his attention to Danny again to continue their conversation.

"Let me show you something. I've been working on this for a long time, but haven't been able to get it quite right, it's actually based off some of your code that I've modified"

Bryan turned back to his console and began to pull up a couple of windows on his three monitors.

"Sorry to interrupt, but would you mind putting up some of the news reports on one of your screens?"

I asked. Bryan gave me a look confirming I was interrupting.

"Good idea Candace, we need to keep our eyes and ears to the ground"

Danny said. Bryan's face changed after he saw Danny's approval. It was like I was the breaking into Bryan's "boys-only clubhouse," but it didn't matter, I wasn't going to let his bad attitude distract me from our mission, this was for Asher; this was for us.

On the furthest screen to the left, Bryan setup a four square of the major news casts turned way down so he could continue talking to Danny as he finished pulling up the programs he wanted to show him. I was reading the news tickers scroll by on the different networks newscasts and shifted my concentration between different news anchor voices.

"Oh no, turn it up, quick"

I said.

"What, which one?"

Bryan asked. I pointed to the screen with the newscasts

"It doesn't matter, they're all reporting the same thing, look."

We all turned our attention as Bryan turned up the volume for one of the news reports. They were all reporting that thousands of people were flooding local hospitals and being treated for severe flu-like symptoms. The actual illness was not known, but all cases were being traced back to people who attended a Yankees game earlier that day. Perfectly healthy people were suddenly coming down with the strange sickness. They were also reporting that all the metro area hospitals and clinics were already over capacity and efforts were underway to setup emergency triage centers at major event centers across the city that were currently being repurposed for FEMA use.

"This is it. It's starting"

Danny said under his breath with a deadpan look on his face.

We watched the reports continue on about initial speculation which quickly turned into confirmation reports. The news reports were all abruptly interrupted by breaking news which cut to an emergency White House press conference that was just getting underway. The press secretary opened the conference by first introducing head of the Center for Disease Control.

The CDC Administrator explained that we as an American people were in immediate danger and were about to experience an epidemic of colossal proportion due to the extremely aggressive nature of the highly contagious disease that had been loosed on the American people.

He went on to explain that he had received intelligence that the source of this deadly disease was secured by Anonymous hacking NanoCell's systems to change the internal security coding of the experimental bio-assest, allowing it to be released into NanoCell's distribution system and auto-shipped out of their own facility. He claimed this contagious airborne strain of super cancer was being developed by scientists at NanoCell in order to further understand it's strange nature but had recently been stolen and weaponized.

He announced that the strain was so new that there had not been an antidote strain developed yet to destroy it, part of why it was so dangerous. He concluded by stating that he had officially advised the president to commence and enforce a complete national quarantine of the American population, effective immediately.

The press secretary then introduced The head of FEMA who went on to explain that all hospitals in the greater metropolitan area were over capacity at this point and that infected individuals have been pouring into the makeshift triages at sports stadiums, schools and other community centers and would also be at capacity soon. He urged individuals to go to their homes and seal themselves in as best as possible using duct tape and plastic garbage bags around their doors and windows to help minimize the spread and infection of the horrible disease around the city.

He mentioned that cases were popping up in other areas of the state as well as out of state and it was only a matter of time before the epidemic had reached full blown proportions.

The head of FEMA then stepped down and was followed again by the press secretary who then introduced the President of the United States.

"My fellow Americans, we are faced with an imminent national danger. An attack on our soil is not something we take lightly. I want to assure you all that the full resources of the United States government are being utilized to bring to justice these terrorists that have committed these heinous and traitorous attacks. Officials in our intelligence communities in the CIA and FBI as well as Homeland Security have all conclusively identified the perpetrators as the cyber terror syndicate Anonymous. Anonymous had previously been believed to be leaderless but new intelligence has confirmed Asher Wry as its leader. Intelligence has also confirmed that the outbreak of the disease had been traced back to a silent bio-bomb that was detonated during our national anthem at the New York Yankees baseball game earlier today. Intel further indicates that 24 more of these deadly bio-bombs have been positioned in heavily populated centers in major cities throughout the world. Efforts to locate their exact locations is underway already but have not yielded any results as of yet. We will contain this threat and act with great expediency to ensure the safety of our citizens. To that end, it is with solemn conviction and unwavering determination to defend and protect the American people that after careful deliberation with White House advisors, the intelligence community and senior military officials that I announce the activation of the advised quarantine order as well as immediate invocation of martial law in the United States of America with the sole intent of enforcing the quarantine and maintaining law and order in the imminent chaos that will be coming in the following hours and days. Asher Wry and Anonymous will be brought to justice and prosecuted using the full resources of the anti-terror act. May God be with us."

The President stepped down and the press secretary followed up the previous statements by telling people to stay tuned as emergency safety instructions and a repeating bullet point message of the governing guidelines of the quarantine and martial law that were immediately taking effect and what was going to happen. We couldn't believe what we had just heard.

We sat there reading the repeating list of restrictions and dangers we had been sentenced to, looking dumbfounded at each other when another attack hit me. My spine seized and arched as I cried out in pain. The burning in my spine soon smoldered, diffusing out into my extremities. It left me drained and feeling lifeless, I could feel the toll that each attack took on my deteriorating body. Danny reached out to hold me up as my muscles relaxed from the tensing and I began to slump over. My body was having trouble supporting itself in spite of the weight loss I experienced while incarcerated at NanoCell. I felt frail, a wisp of my former self in this weakened state.

Danny asked Bryan

"Do you have anything to eat, maybe that will help, something sweet to raise her blood sugar, anything."

Bryan went to the kitchen and returned with a handful of snack cakes and caffeinated sodas.

"This is all I have at the moment, I usually order in."

Danny took one of the sodas and cracked it open, offering it to me almost like an infant bottle. Even though I was low on pride, I still had enough strength left to take the soda from him and take a few sips myself before holding it out for Danny to take it and set it down on the desk for me. He handed me one of the chocolate snack cakes and proceeded to help wipe the fresh blood that had appeared under my neck wounds again after this attack. I ate the cake slowly at first, then graduating to ravenously fast by the third one. I took another drink and felt marginally better. The sugar boost helped perk me up although the lingering ache in my spine and nerves was a constant reminder that things were going to get worse before they got better.

Danny seemed to be managing his pain well, but he had a fading look in his eyes. The lies purported in the press conference were only a vehicle to stall people and scare them into submission until armed military personal could be put in place and Asher's sensationalized capture could be broadcast after Conrad had gotten the starskin from Asher. We we're unsure of how true the reports were of the other 24 bio-bombs around the world, but we weren't about to take any chances that Conrad was bluffing and no one knew exactly how much time was left before such a globally scaled attack would take place.

There was a noticeable roar of panicked noise that had ramped up sharply following the White House press conference. Bryan moved the curtains away from the window behind his monitors.

"People are going crazy out there. Everyone is just leaving their cars, it's complete gridlock, their covering their faces with their shirts and running down the street."

Danny and I stood up to confirm what we were hearing. My heart sank to see everyone so scared, running for shelter to save themselves. We sat back down slowly. We looked at each other then back to the screens in front of us. Everyone had a grim look on their face.

By now, one of the monitors had an interface with a well-endowed Japanese school girl crudely displayed in ascii characters who was winking at us and a caption bubble with her saying "S.I.B.A." The other monitor had line after tedious line of software code. Bryan broke the uncomfortable silence in the room somewhat callously

"As I was saying, meet SIBA: Sophisticated Internal Blivet Algorithm. It's the future of hacking, well in theory anyway. It goes beyond standard anamorphic methods of simply disguising code, elements or resources, it intelligently learns how to become them.

The algorithm is presented with an expectation when trying to access a database or network, learns what the system needs to allow access and becomes that element whether it be a file, a password or script. I've tested it successfully on low level systems, but I've been having trouble with some of the newer encryption standards some government and high tech corporate systems have been implementing lately. The deep encryption changes millions of times per second, even with all this equipment, I can't come close to getting up to that speed to even attempt to lock onto to an encryption point, let alone decrypt it quickly enough before the encryption changes again millions of times."

"Hahahaha"

Danny burst out into a loud and enthusiastic laughter.

"I didn't show you this to be mocked!"

Bryan immediately became flustered and angry.

"No, no, no. Are you kidding? This is amazing! This is exactly what we need"

Danny said.

"But it's only a toy without the decryption element"

Bryan said pessimistically.

"Who says we don't have that? That's why I laughed; it's amazing that you've developed something so ingenious like this. Decryption is the easy part. I led the development in the new encryption standard through my company Codeworm."

"I didn't know you were affiliated with them"

Bryan said.

"I'm not; I'm unofficially the silent owner. Given my track record, the licensing deals would have never gone so smoothly if the government and other companies I've had run-ins with in the past knew that I was involved. I provide the backbone for all of our special projects then basically hand them off to our engineers for beta-testing; they just send any bugs back to the totally separate development department, that's me. Anyway, the beauty isn't in the complexity of the encryption, it's in the simplicity. The trick is to isolate a single point in the encryption and loop it essentially which causes it to invert itself and open up. Well, there's more to it, but that's the gist of it in theory. Do you mind if I take a look?"

Bryan happily moved aside

"By all means."

Danny scooted his chair up closer to the console, but when he tried to sit up to correct his posture in the chair, his torso jolted forward in the chair and his head slammed backward. He let out a muffled growl and grabbed for the back of his neck.

"Oh man, both of you?"

Bryan said rhetorically as he reached for another wet wipe for him. I took the wet wipe from Bryan in one hand and put my palm on Danny's back and rubbed it lightly back and forth

"It's ok, just focus, deep breaths."

He seemed to be responding better than I was to the pain or at least disguising it better. He rested his head forward and began slowly massaging his temples with his thumb and middle finger. I reached up to his neck he was still holding tightly to and softly touched his hand with the wet wipe to let him know I was trying to get in to help wipe his wound and clean the blood. He clinched it tighter and I recoiled.

I tried again after a second, this time lightly touching the back of his hand with my fingertips. The tight grip of his hand immediately began to loosen and he slowly lifted it off. It looked really bad, much worse than I anticipated. I could see deep into his skin; seeing Danny's puncture wounds made mine begin to ache sympathetically. I finished carefully wiping the blood from around the holes in his neck and he finished wiping his hand with another wipe from Bryan. Danny loudly exhaled a deep breath

"Ok, let's hope those don't become habit ay?"

Danny's humor, dry as it was, helped break the tension in the room as he picked up where he was and began scanning through the thousands of line of code in Bryan's software. He seemed very familiar with what he was looking at, browsing through it like a children's book and approving sections under his breath until he came to a section in the code where stopped to examine it in more detail.

"Yep, right there"

Bryan said. Danny looked over it carefully for a few minutes.

"Ya, I can see why you a hit a brick wall approaching it this way."

Danny said. Bryan looked at him confused and a bit irritated

"but it's the only way that makes any kind of sense, we just need fast enough hardware."

Danny smiled back at Bryan.

"That's like cross training to try to outrun the speed of light. Hang on, let me shell in to my server and grab something." Danny opened another blank window and typed several commands over the next few minutes; we were all intently focused on what Danny was doing. The cursor was left blinking at the bottom of the screen. Danny turned to Bryan

"I need your root"

"No way"

Bryan was quick to shoot him down.

"What's your root?"

I asked.

"Seriously?"

Bryan looked at me like I was asking what color the sky was, I felt stupid for asking but Danny shot him a look right back. Bryan explained

"It's the master user for the entire server, root can access and do anything on the server."

"Do you want your software to actually work or do you want to leave it neutered?"

Danny said.

"Look, you're the ones that need the help here, I'm fine pushing along as is"

Bryan wasn't budging.

"Really? I don't believe that, not for a second. Holding out isn't going to do you or anyone any good when the infection spreads to us. Here, I'll trade you ok? An eye for an eye. You don't even have to give it to me, just type it in, in trade I'll write mine down for you to guarantee the armistice"

Bryan's smirk gave way to a sideways smile. I was shocked at how selfish and close-minded Bryan was being; with so much at stake including his life, he was worried about giving out his server's password. He handed Danny a pen and a small notepad.

"You first."

Danny took the pen and notepad and jotted down a long password made of every variety of characters and numbers on the keyboard and handed it back to Bryan.

"Ok, turn around"

Danny turned his chair around to face me. He just smiled at me calmly as Bryan typed in his equally ridiculous password. I smiled back at Danny. It was only a moment, but it felt nice to rest and take a deep, human breath.

"Thank you"

I said quietly.

"Ok"

Bryan said as he finished typing. Danny turned back around to the waiting cursor and hit enter. Danny typed a few more commands and waited for the results. He kept typing a few more commands after waiting for each command to complete. Danny worked at editing Bryan's software for the next few hours, trying to integrate the encryption algorithm into the software. It was trial and error, but Danny was nothing if not determined.

I had asked Bryan for his notepad and a pen so I could try to make some notes on what I wanted to say in my message, if we ever had the chance to broadcast it. I felt nauseous thinking of what to say in a time like this. I felt like a chaplain who was assigned to administer last rights to an entire mortally wounded army on his first day. Hope was hard to find in this darkness with so many sick and dying.

We continued random checks at the chaos unfolding in the streets below while Danny widdled away line after line of code trying to get it working correctly. In between window checks we kept glued to the endless stream of negative news reports detail outlandish stories of desperate attempts by people to gather supplies in an effort to seal themselves inside their homes and survive for an indeterminate amount of time. People were looting, fighting and even killing for the last of the suddenly invaluable supplies listed on the emergency broadcast reports.

As hours passed the streets outside grew quieter. For the most part, people had holed themselves away in their homes by now and a dark and eerie calm fell over most parts of the city.

International news reports showed the same kind of panic was happening in cities all over the world and many countries around the world had taken similar measures to invoke and enforce martial law in preparation for the imminent mass infection. Reports of the disease already starting to spread internationally from the initial Yankee stadium infection were being broadcast along with gory details of the rapid phases the infected individual would undergo.

Initial symptoms of the disease included a flu-like onset, coughing, lethargy, swollen throat and eyes. The telltale sign of infection was the red circles around the victim's eyes due to blood pooling around the eye sockets. By the time the area around their eyes had become red and swollen, the person would generally not live more than two hours or so before the victim's body was completely ravaged by the undiscerning disease. The infected person experienced excruciating pain starting from the spine out through every nerve ending in the body before each organ slowly shut down eventually killing the person via complete organ failure.

All the news channels showed the same widely distributed time lapse treatment of a patient that went through the person being initially admitted to a local hospital earlier in the day, the development of the inflamed red rings around his eyes and his death only hours later. The media had affectionately dubbed the deadly disease "Red Ring." There was no hope for anyone who contracted Red Ring. It was airborne and spreading like wildfire now. I grabbed Danny who was only half listening to the news reports

"Let me see you"

I demanded. I was relieved to discover Danny did not have the red rings around his eyes.

"Look at my eyes, do I have them?"

I could see my look of terror reflecting from his face.

"No you don't have them, you're fine."

I let go of his shirt and he went back to coding.

"I'm sorry"

I let out a frustrated sigh. He turned back for a moment and looked at me.

"It's ok, we're ok."

We exchanged slight, but honest smiles and turned back to his coding.

~

Ch. 10
| crown |

As I slowly forced my eyes open, I found myself looking straight down at the blood that was pooling from my face. Regaining consciousness, I glanced in my peripheral vision to notice each of my wrists being suspended by steel cables that were both restraining me and holding my badly beaten body vertically. The sting of his telescoping metal cane spread from the impact line across my face to the sides and back of my head before slowly burning down my spine and throughout the rest of my body.

The room was bright white and not unlike the cell I had saved Candace and Danny from earlier. Only my spattered blood on the floor and walls disrupted the pristine sterility. I could hear the slow pacing of boots behind me. A pair of knobby black boots and BDU's entered my field of vision, stopping directly in front of the pool of blood. I was too weak to look up at the face of my assailant but noticed his patch said "VINCENT." I felt a breath-taking blow to the stomach from the swift knee to the gut followed by another down striking on the top of my head with the metal cane.

I couldn't make any sound or movements. I just hung there suspended in agonizing pain. I couldn't contain the blood and saliva from falling out of my mouth.

"You know your little princess and the hack are dead right?"

he began laughing.

"What, you don't find that funny?"

he mocked. He waited a moment, grabbed me by the hair and ripped my head up.

"Look at me while I'm talkin' to you boy!"

I could barely focus on his face as even the muscles of my eyes were weak and sore. I didn't know how long I had been here or how long I had been beaten, but it felt like I had been broken in every place in my body. A voice emitted from the walls

"Long time no see Asher. We seem to keep missing each other at those festive protests you and your friends like to host on my property. I have to tolerate the public crybaby parties to a point, but in my castle, I am king. You took something very valuable of mine Asher and it's time you give it back. I may not know everything about that skin, but I know as its owner, it can be forced to leave a host if the host does not will it there."

My body weight was putting intense pressure on my wrists inside the restraints and I could barely focus on every few words the voice was saying, but it persisted.

"I'm ordering you to reject the skin, that you actively will it out of you."

The voice paused for a moment as if waiting for compliance of some kind. Commander Vincent was still circling around me standing by as a physical insurance policy to reinforce what the voice was saying. When I failed to speak or produce the starskin, I received a swift reminder in the form of the metal cane to my already aching knees. They buckled beneath me again, stretching and compressing the skin around my raw wrists.

~

Bryan had his neck kinked forward like a bird and was muttering to himself in self-loathing amazement as he watched Danny code. I was entranced and staring into a coma-like blur recalling Asher smiling back at me on the morning that I was taken from the subway station. His face was eclipsing the morning light, allowing only the brilliant white rays to shine and crown around his face. It was an endless memory loop in my mind that kept repeating.

"Candace, are you ok?"

Danny's voice broke my focus

"Hmm, sorry, I'm fine"

I shook my head hard in an attempt to make myself more alert from the heavy daydream loop I was stuck in. I turned my focus back to the news reports that were currently showing massive overcrowding of people in various facilities around the country that were waiting out the inevitable while following up that report with contrasting news that the vast majority of our nation's government had been accounted for at specially prepared facilities to ensure that our government could continue to operate smoothly and effectively throughout the duration of this national emergency.

"What a farce! How can they even justify reporting that? Showing stadiums full of people who will all be dead within the next few hours while assuring us that our fearless leaders and their families are safe in their overstocked fortified shelters, like that's supposed to make anyone feel any better about the end of nearly all human life on the planet!"

Bryan was so worked up that he was spitting on the monitors as he ranted. The terror in people's eyes was heartbreakingly genuine, it echoed in the pit of my stomach.

Outside Bryan's window came a long, howling siren that decimated the silence as it effortlessly cut through anything and everything. It was a concrete reminder of the desperation that surrounded us all. I closed my eyes again trying to get back to my loop, but he was gone. I was left with my pain.

Each of my nerve attacks had taken a numbing toll which was slowly spreading through my body. I could still move, but it was slow going and I felt week everywhere.

"Yes! Finally"

Danny yelled out as he typed another set of commands. Bryan shot up correcting his horrible slouch. Danny looked at Bryan with a confident smirk and hit enter, not breaking eye contact as he did it. All four squares on the third monitor flashed from displaying their dismal news reports to displaying identical images of a baby lamb. We all broke out into cheering and excited laughter.

"A lamb?"

Bryan said.

"What, he's kinda cute."

We all laughed again until the Danny and Bryan both looked at me. The weight of their eyes was heavy and reminded me that it was my turn. Bryan took over configuring a webcam which was shortly online and waiting for me. I took a deep breath in, my lungs fluttered like I'd been crying hard for the past long while. I closed my eyes and exhaled cleanly. Danny and Bryan both stood up to give me some space. Danny angled the camera to focus on me as Bryan waited for the go ahead to make the stream live.

I was stalling to make sure everything was in place. I moved to adjust myself into a more relaxed position. I sat up straight and took another deep breath, as I did this, the pain exploded out of my numb spine and funneling out to every nerve in my body. I collapsed on the floor, violently recoiling my arms and legs. I couldn't breathe or speak. I just lay there helplessly experiencing my broken body shutting down in a hyper aware mental state.

I was crying although I couldn't produce any tears. Danny and Bryan stood by helpless to do anything to help me

"We've gotta do something"

Bryan was panicked.

"What do you suggest, take her to the hospital, so we can all get Red Ring?"

Danny snapped back rhetorically.

"They should only last a few seconds"

"Then why isn't she stopping?"

Bryan asked. After a few more seconds, my body finally let go of the painful tension. My arms and legs were lifeless in front of me. Laying down even felt exhausting. After a few minutes of focused breathing, Bryan and Danny slowly and carefully reached around me and lifted me into the chair again. They propped me up in Bryan's bigger chair with some blankets and pillows so I could sit up and not fall out.

Danny helped wipe the blood from my neck and Bryan left the room. I could tell it was worse now, there a lot more blood than before and it took several wipes to clean it up and it just kept coming. Bryan looked at Danny like a statue seeing the growing pile of bloody wipes when he returned from grabbing a bigger rag to help soak up the blood and to put pressure on the open wounds.

Danny folded the clean white rag into a smaller rectangle. Bryan passed a roll of medical tape to Danny which he used to secure the rag to my neck like a medical collar. My eyelids were feeling heavy and my breathing was shallow. I looked up at Danny and then to Bryan and nodded as I slowly blinked.

~

The seamless blood spattered wall suddenly opened up and I was being approached by a fast and steady pace. My head was ripped back by Commander Vincent and I was standing face to face with the voice now. Conrad's eyes were almost totally dilated as he starred at me with a dark coldness. He was an imposing figure filled with deep emptiness, but he wasn't getting inside me. He threatened

"You *will* give me the skin, if I have to cut it out of your lifeless body"

I half-chuckled with the little energy I had left and immediately received a reminder that that was not ok from Commander Vincent's cane to my other knee. My chuckle quickly turning into a wincing sentence

"You're wrong; I can't just will it from me. *It* chose me, not the other way around"

Conrad was furious. He lunged for Commander Vincent's boot knife and ripped my shirt open in the same raging motion and held the knife millimeters from my chest. His hand was shaking with anger, sneering his clinched teeth like an alpha wolf. He moved closer to me while keeping the knife to my chest. I could feel the heat escaping his aggressive whispers as he spoke close to my face

"The skin is *mine*, you shouldn't even know it exists. People like you are a disease, killing and defiling everything of beauty in this world. You should have been eradicated a long time ago. There's no room for human scum like you on this earth, on *my* earth. If it wasn't for a certain traitorous daughter of mine having developed a pension for bottom feeders like you, none of us would be in this position. You'd be out there with probably a few more worthless hours left before the Red Ring got to you. Nasty little virus, it's a shame you'll miss out on that one. You see, only the worst kind of people attract the worst kinds of things to them. The fact that you're about to die should tell you something about the kind of scum you are"

~

When I opened my eyes, I could see myself in all the four square spaces on the last monitor and I couldn't hide the tears in my voice when I said

"Hi. My name is Candace. I'm not sure what to say. I need your help. We all need your help. I know you're scared; I'm scared too, but I made a promise. I made a promise to my friend, to Asher. When I was a little girl, I liked pretending. I liked trying on my mother's clothes and pretending I was a princess on her way to the ball. My mother was furious the first time she caught me in her closet. To teach me a lesson, she locked her six year old daughter in the dark closet for two days without food or water. Even after almost 20 years, I haven't ever forgotten that. Cold moments like that freeze in time, inside us. Over and over, the cold and snow packs down freezing us to the bone. Ice builds up over time and cracks our hardened hearts. I've felt cold my whole life, like a drifting iceberg too far north to melt, even in full sun light. There was never any warmth in my parent's light. I'm so grateful I'm finally warm, which is very ironic given how cold I am right now, hehe. Asher has warmed me through my core. My thoughts are like warm waves crashing all through me. In my memories, I'm not scared anymore, I'm not alone anymore, he's right there next to me with his arm around me, smiling. He's telling me everything's going to be alright, and it is. Everything's going to be..."

~

"Candace? Candace! No no no no."

I was distracted from the steam of Conrad's mineral breath by a sudden overwhelming surge of aether that washed through me completely, igniting me. The shield dropped and everything opened up around me.

I immediately sensed Candace; her light was slipping away as the lights went black all over NanoCell.

I was the only light that came back into the room, shining like radiant liquid-plasma flames, I emanated a crystalline light that far surpassed the previously white out lights in the room. The white light refracted all the colors of the spectrum through each other.

Conrad and Commander Vincent cowered back, their eyes growing with terror with every step I took toward them. Conrad miss stepped, landing flat on his back. I peered deep into his eyes; there was no light left to reflect in side of him. I looked away from him stoically and slipped out of the cell, securing it with a thought as I left.

I was racing through the aether, over the earth, water and ice. I passed through the earth's northern opening, passing directly into the inner sun. The earth's heart was synced with mine and I felt the love pumping through its heart into mine. I felt the peoples' love that rushed into its heart that manifested the prayer

236

I had nested there. Candace's heart was also in sync, but it was fluttering and growing weak with every beat.

I was alone inside of the heart. I fell to my knees with both palms flat on the base of the heart. I synced with the heart and focused my love on the singularity of everything. In that singularity I felt a familiar unified light rise up from that singularity which passed through my body like a conduit into the base of the inner sun before being blasted out of the aether, the heart's omnipresent nervous system.

The EMP-like blast of pure light came full circle *from* its source *back* to its source, resonating harmoniously through everything; I was the resonant.

The intelligently powerful pulse had sealed the safe rooms that were housing the corrupt politicians and their corporate employers; electronically and eternally sealed in their elite tombs. It sealed the Draconians in their hive-like network of bases in the earth's crust. By the time the pulse went out, so was Candace's last flicker of light.

I lifted my hands from the heart and found Vasha standing before me. I felt the sincere depth of her empathy flowing through me. She smiled at me softly

"Thank you Asher, go to her."

She walked forward and disappeared inside me. I gasped as I felt her pass through me into the singularity.

I immediately slipped into the room of computers where Danny and Bryan were frantically checking her for a pulse. I scooped her into my arms and slipped us both back into the earth's heart. I was cradling her delicate, lifeless body in my arms as I knelt with her, my tears soaking her pale face, pleading for her life.

"No, you can't go, I won't let you, I won't let you!"

I frantically wiped my tears from her porcelain face. I pressed my forehead to hers; my face so close to hers, they touched as I shook deeply. I kissed her lips softly and held her tight against me. I closed my eyes slowly, hoping to feel our hearts sync again, but her rhythm was gone.

Suddenly a frequency focused into being, giving rise to its Solfeggio light form of being, followed by another and another until all six Solfeggios were once again harmonizing in perfect unison, triggering the seventh and final harmonic of divine white light, transfiguring Candace and I into perfected energy. Our consciousness became whole in the unifying singularity. The aether flowed freely throughout us and we within it.

The pure essence of love resonated omnisciently through the aether, cleansing the intentions of the hearts of mankind and restoring wholeness to their disease ravaged bodies. The fear and darkness in our hearts was gone, leaving only perfected human intent to refract forward through our future.

We were lying in the middle of the Feathergrass fields, looking up at the iridescently illuminated sun, feeling it beating in sync with our hearts. We watched as inner earth's skyline transformed into an intriguingly Escheresque optical illusion. The Atlantian craft moved in tight yet fluid formation in relation to each other like buoys on the sea as they moved out of inner earth.

On the surface the same gathering was happening with the surface-side ships, they were all coming out of hiding across the globe, filling the skies of nearly every major city in the world. They were all converging in the ionosphere over earth's northern polar opening.

Vasha spoke in a whisper that escaped no living thing. Everything was calm and every word was heard.

"We have been with you long, safing your harbors and guarding your keep until one arose, the one that would bring you into the singularity. You have arrived well-traveled as we depart, ever vigil."

The last of the Atlantian battalion were in their rendezvous place before Vasha finished speaking. They paused for only a moment before vanishing, leaving two last words hanging in the air

"in love"

resonating in a pure harmonic sustain.

The tall Feathergrass was bending slowly above us in the gentle breeze. I looked down toward Candace and said

"Always together."

Candace looked up from my chest and met me smiling

"Always as one."

www.ingramcontent.com/pod-product-compliance
Lightning Source LLC
Chambersburg PA
CBHW030428290526
45786CB00001B/194